# THE SIMPLE SPEAKING FRENCH WORKBOOK FOR BEGINNERS

SARENA VAQUEZAS

# INTRODUCTION

If you've ever dreamed of having a conversation beneath the twinkling lights of the Eiffel Tower, or ordered a fresh croissant in a local bakery by the Seine, then you're at the right starting point. Welcome to "The Simple Speaking French Workbook for Beginners". This workbook is designed to guide you from knowing little to no French to confidently holding basic conversations and understanding essential phrases.

At the heart of every language lies the desire to communicate, to understand and to be understood. French, with its rich history, culture, and undeniable charm, has captured the hearts of many. Whether you're learning French for a trip, for school, for business, or just for the sheer pleasure of it, this book promises to make your journey both enjoyable and rewarding.

The title may hint that this is all about simplicity, and that's our primary goal – to uncomplicate the process of learning French. But simplicity does not imply that the journey won't be profound and enriching.

Let's delve into a brief overview of what to expect:

Chapter 1: It all starts with Bonjour – An essential greeting that transcends beyond a simple "hello". This chapter sets the tone, introducing you to basic greetings that pave the way for the initial, simple conversations.

Chapter 2: All about you – Dive into self-introduction, and learn how to share more about who you are and your interests.

Chapter 3: I speak a little French – Conquer the hesitation of speaking by mastering phrases that express your proficiency and eagerness to learn.

Chapter 4: This is not a pipe – An intriguing title inspired by Magritte's famous painting. Here, we'll touch upon perception, objects, and descriptions, giving you tools to talk about the world around you.

Chapter 5: How may I help you? – Venture into the realms of seeking and offering assistance, ensuring you're always ready to lend a hand or ask for directions.

Chapter 6: One big happy family – Understand family dynamics in French, introducing and talking about family members and relationships.

Chapter 7: A city dweller – Dive into urban life and familiarize yourself with places, directions, and city attractions.

Chapter 8: The ball's in your court! – Engage in recreation, sports, and hobbies, ensuring you can share your pastime activities and join in the local fun.

Chapter 9: Beyond baguettes – French isn't just about the Eiffel Tower or croissants. This chapter explores the cultural nuances and richness, helping you appreciate and talk about the lesser-known gems.

Chapter 10: No rain check allowed – Master the art of making plans, confirming appointments, and ensuring you never miss a date.

Chapter 11: The hands of time – Time is of the essence. Learn to talk about time, days, and dates.

Chapter 12: An ordinary day – Walk through a day in the life of a typical French local, from morning routines to nightly rituals.

Chapter 13: How about a drink? – Explore the vibrant French café culture, ordering drinks, and engaging in casual chit-chat.

Chapter 14: The art of French dining – Delve into the delectable world of French cuisine, learning how to order, appreciate, and discuss food.

Chapter 15: At the crossroads – Equip yourself with navigational language, be it for road trips or strolling through winding streets.

Chapter 16: Ready for an adventure – For the travelers at heart, this chapter focuses on vacations, explorations, and discoveries.

Chapter 17: A thing of the past – Delve deeper into the language, exploring past tenses and discussing memories.

Chapter 18: The adventure continues – A peek into advanced conversations and building your fluency for the road ahead.

Lastly, the Vocabulary Lists by Theme will be your constant companion, categorizing essential words and phrases for quick reference.

Remember, every new word learned, every sentence spoken, brings you one step closer to fluency. It's a journey of a thousand miles that begins with a single "Bonjour." By the end of this workbook, you won't just be reading and writing French; you'll be speaking it with confidence. Dive in with enthusiasm, practice regularly, and let the beauty of the French language unfold before you.

French is often referred to as the "language of love," and as you navigate the chapters of this workbook, you'll soon understand why. The rhythmic flow, the elegant structure, and the expressive nature of the language captivate the listener, enveloping them in a melodious embrace.

As you embark on this educational voyage, it's essential to remember the reasons that drew you to the French language. Perhaps it was the allure of the French Riviera, the romantic streets of Paris, or the culinary delights of Bordeaux. Or maybe it was the rich tapestry of French literature, art, and cinema. Whatever your motivation, hold onto it tightly, as it will be the beacon that illuminates your path, especially during challenging moments.

The design of this workbook follows a strategic progression, ensuring you'll first ground yourself in the basics before branching out into more complex topics. We've integrated practical situations you might encounter, from ordering at a bistro to discussing the weather or navigating the Paris metro.

However, while this book offers a structured approach to learning, the key to mastery lies within you. Here are a few tips to enhance your learning experience:

Practice Regularly: Like any skill, consistency is crucial. Even if it's just a few minutes daily, regular practice can significantly boost retention and confidence.

Engage in Active Learning: Don't just read and listen; speak! The more you practice speaking, the faster you'll feel at ease with the language.

Immerse Yourself: Surround yourself with French as much as possible. Listen to French music, watch French movies, or try reading simple French books or articles.

Connect with Native Speakers: Engaging in conversations with native speakers can offer invaluable practice. Platforms like language exchange websites can help in this endeavor.

Be Kind to Yourself: Learning a new language is a journey with highs and lows. Celebrate the small victories and don't get disheartened by the occasional stumbles.

The beauty of learning French – or any language, for that matter – is not just in the ability to communicate in a foreign tongue but in the doors it opens for you. You'll gain access to new cultures, perspectives, friendships, and experiences that were previously beyond reach. And as you progress, you'll not just be decoding words and sentences, but also the rich tapestry of French history, its art, its music, and its heart.

With "The Simple Speaking French Workbook for Beginners," you hold not just a guide to the French language but also a passport to a world of new possibilities. So, as you turn the pages and dive into the chapters, remember that each word, each phrase, each lesson is a stepping stone to a world that awaits your discovery.

To conclude this introduction, I'd like to borrow a famous

French saying – "C'est en forgeant qu'on devient forgeron." In essence, it means "practice makes perfect." Keep forging ahead, and soon the nuances of French will become second nature to you.

Joyeux apprentissage! (Happy Learning!)

# CONTENTS

# Chapter 1: It all starts with Bonjour

*Bonjour, bonsoir, merci, sont trois règles de la vie.*

*Good day, good evening, thank you, are the three rules of life.*

- a Breton proverb

*Bonjour* (Hello, Good day) is one of those words you will hear a lot when you go to France. It is an essential word to start a conversation, both formal and informal. When asking for directions, for example, you might start with a polite *Bonjour*. When entering a store, the post office, an elevator, or a restaurant, there's nothing more native-like than greeting with this expression. There is thus no better way to start your journey than by learning this word.

In the first part of this chapter, you will learn commonly used expressions to greet someone and say goodbye. And then, we will teach you how to introduce yourself or ask how someone is. *On y va !* Let's go!

## Greetings

The French language distinguishes between formal and informal situations. As the name suggests, a formal situation demands the use of more polite expressions. Formal situations include talking to a stranger and addressing people in professional or commercial situations (for example, speaking to your boss or to a shop owner). On the other hand, informal situations include talking to your friends and family, to close colleagues and classmates, or to children.

One must keep in mind the difference between these two situations when greeting someone. Another consideration to make is the time of the day. For instance, there are four ways one can say "hello" depending on the social context and time:

| *Bonjour* | Means "hello" or "good day".<br>Used in both formal and informal situations. |
| --- | --- |

| | |
|---|---|
| | Used all day until around 6 p.m. |
| *Bonsoir* | Means "good evening".<br>Used in both formal and informal situations.<br>Used from 6 p.m. onwards. |
| *Salut* | Means "hello" and "bye".<br>Used uniquely in informal situations.<br>Used any time of the day. |
| *Coucou* | Means "hi".<br>Very informal and playful.<br>Used any time of the day. |

Let us put this in context. Say, you are entering a bakery, you would say *Bonjour*. You meet a group of friends in a coffee shop, you might say *Salut*. You text a very close friend, you write *Coucou*. You dine at a restaurant in the evening, you will greet the waiters with *Bonsoir*.

**CULTURE TIP**
***To kiss or not to kiss?***

Cheek-kissing is an important part of French culture. It is called *faire la bise* (v. give a kiss on the cheek) and is done when saying hello or bidding someone goodbye. It might be difficult to grasp the etiquette in the beginning. Here are some reminders to avoid a greeting faux pas:

- It is common for friends and family to *faire la bise*.
- It is common to *faire la bise* among young adults when introduced to a friend of a friend.
- It is common between two women or between a man and a woman.
- Between two men, unless family or very close friends, it is less common.
- Kissing two cheeks (each side) is most typical.
- In Southern France, it is common to do three *bises* (left, right then left again for example).

- A few regions do up to *five bises*!

A good rule of thumb – and this is true for every cultural aspect of the language – is of course to let the French native lead. If the person inclines his or her head towards you, you'd know that you are about to *faire la bise*.

# Saying goodbye

Like greetings, parting expressions also vary according to the social setting. Some can be used at any time of the day:

| *Au revoir* | Means "goodbye".<br>Used in both formal and informal situations. |
|---|---|
| *Salut* | Means "bye".<br>Used in informal situations. |

Others may be used whatever the social setting, but at a specific time of the day:

| *Bonne journée* | Have a good day |
|---|---|
| *Bon après-midi* | Have a good afternoon |
| *Bonne fin de journée* | Have a good day's end<br>(used mostly when the day is about to end) |
| *Bonne soirée* | Have a good evening |
| *Bonne nuit* | Good night |

Or, if you are expecting to see somebody again, you can also say:

| *À tout de suite* | See you in a moment |
|---|---|
| *À tout à l'heure* | See you in a bit |
| *À bientôt* | See you soon |
| *À plus* (inf.) | See you later |

| | |
|---|---|
| *À plus tard* | |
| *À demain* | See you tomorrow |
| *À la prochaine* | Until next time |

You might be familiar with the expression *Adieu*, which also means goodbye. Note, however, that this is rarely used and is a form of grim farewell. *Adieu* means you will never see the person again. In fact, it is so final it literally translates to "To God"! It is thus best to avoid using this expression unless you are definitively cutting ties with someone.

## First meetings

Let's look at this short dialogue between Pierre and Hélène who are meeting each other for the first time.

| | |
|---|---|
| **Pierre** : *Bonjour.* | Hello. |
| **Hélène** : *Bonjour.* | Hello. |
| **Pierre** : *Comment vous appelez-vous ?* | What is your name? |
| **Hélène** : *Je m'appelle Hélène, et vous ?* | My name is Hélène, and you? |
| **Pierre** : *Je m'appelle Pierre. Enchanté.* | My name is Pierre. Nice to meet you. |
| **Hélène** : *Enchantée, Pierre.* | Nice to meet you, Pierre. |

### Asking one's name

To ask someone's name, you can say *Comment vous appelez-vous ?* like Pierre did. Or, you can also use the variation *Vous vous appelez comment ?* Both of these phrases are for formal situations. In casual situations you can say *Comment tu t'appelles ?* or *Tu t'appelles comment ?*

We know, that looks like a bunch of alien words with some odd repetitions. So let's break this down. *Comment vous appelez-vous ?* literally translates to "How do you call yourself?":

Comment | vous | appelez-vous ?
***How (do) | you | call yourself?***

The variation is in fact just a simple inversion:

Vous | vous appelez | comment ?
***You | call yourself | how?***

*Vous* refers to the pronoun "you". It is used in formal situations or when addressing two or more people. For example, when you want to ask the names of two people, even in informal situations, you would use *vous*.

As for the informal way of asking one's name, we use *tu* instead of *vous*.

Comment | tu | t'appelles ?
***How (do) | you | call yourself?***

Again, we can invert this phrase:

Tu | t'appelles | comment ?
***You | call yourself | how?***

Use *tu* when asking the name of someone your age or someone who is much younger. Also, if you are introduced to a friend of a friend, it is very natural to use the pronoun *tu*.

### Introducing yourself

Now, to introduce yourself, you say *Je m'appelle*… (lit. "I call myself…"), followed by your first name. In the dialogue above, we saw the use of this phrase:

- ***Je m'appelle*** *Hélène.*
- ***Je m'appelle*** *Pierre.*

An alternative, more informal way of introducing yourself is by using the expression *Moi, c'est*… (lit. "Me, it's…"), followed again by your first name.

- ***Moi, c'est*** *Hélène.*
- ***Moi, c'est*** *Pierre.*

Finally, once names are exchanged, one usually says "Nice to meet you" or *Enchanté(e)* in French. For male speakers, it is written simply as *Enchanté*. For female speakers, it is written with an extra *–e*, as in *Enchantée*. Both are pronounced the same way.

### Introducing someone else

To introduce someone else, we use the verb *s'appeler* as well. Note that *il* refers to the pronoun "he", and *elle* to the pronoun "she".

***Il s'appelle*** *Marc.*

His name is Marc. (lit. He calls himself Marc.)

**_Elle s'appelle_** _Lucile._
Her name is Lucile.

When introducing two or more people, we use the pronoun "they". In French, there are two words for "they", _ils_ and _elles_. As you might have guessed, it has to do with the gender of the subject referred to. _Ils_ refers to a masculine "they", while _elles_ refers to a feminine "they".

**_Ils s'appellent_** _Marc et Jean._
Their names are Marc and Jean. (lit. They call themselves Marc and Jean.)

**_Elles s'appellent_** _Lucile et Véronique._
Their names are Lucile and Véronique.

If referring to a group of people with both male and female subjects, we use _ils_ as the neutral pronoun. And so, for instance:

**_Ils s'appellent_** _Clara et Arthur._
Their names are Clara and Arthur.

You can also indicate your relationship to the person you are introducing, using the word _voici_. For example:

**_Voici mon ami,_** _Arthur._
This is my friend, Arthur.

**_Voici ma collègue,_** _Clara_
This is my colleague, Clara.

**_Voici mes amis,_** _Jules et Sophie._
These are my friends, Jules and Sophie.

---

**GRAMMAR TIP**
**The verb _s'appeler_**

By now, you must be familiar with the verb _s'appeler_, used especially in indicating or asking one's name. Like in many languages, French verbs are conjugated. This means that they change according to the subject. We've seen all of these combinations previously, except for _nous_ which refers to the pronoun "we".

| s'appeler | |
|---|---|
| **Je** | m'appelle |
| **Tu** | t'appelles |
| **Il/Elle** | s'appelle |
| **Nous** | nous appelons |
| **Vous** | vous appelez |
| **Ils/Elles** | s'appellent |

You've probably noticed that the verb is composed of two parts, both of which change during conjugation. We will learn more about this kind of verb later on.

Here's a bonus tip for pronunciation: the words *appelle, appelles, appellent* are actually pronounced the exact same way: /ah-pehl/

# Exchanging niceties

Pierre and Hélène meet each other for a second time. Let's look at how their conversation would go.

| | | |
|---|---|---|
| **Pierre** : *Bonjour Hélène.* | | Hello Hélène. |
| **Hélène** : *Bonjour Pierre.* | | Hello Pierre. |
| **Pierre** : *Comment allez-vous ?* | | How are you? |
| **Hélène** : *Je vais bien, merci, et vous ?* | | I'm fine, thank you, and you? |
| **Pierre** : *Très bien, merci.* | | Very well, thank you. |

### Asking how someone is

There are a number of ways to ask "How are you?" in French. Like Pierre, you can say *Comment allez-vous ?,* which is a formal variation. Others include:

- *Vous allez bien ?*
- *Tu vas bien ?*
- *Comment ça va ?*

- *Ça va ?*

The last three are used in informal situations. Remember, as we discussed above, that *tu* is the informal "you". We use *vous* in formal situations or when addressing two or more people.

### Indicating how you are

To respond, you can use these expressions:

| | |
|---|---|
| *Comment allez-vous ?* <br> *Vous allez bien ?* <br> *Tu vas bien ?* | *Je vais bien.* (I'm fine, I'm doing well.) <br> *Je vais très bien.* (I'm doing very well.) |
| *Comment ça va ?* <br> *Ça va ?* | *Oui, ça va.* (Yes, I'm fine.) <br> *Ça va.* (I'm fine.) <br> *Ça va bien.* (I'm fine.) |

Don't forget that you can also ask back the question by saying, "And you?", which is *Et vous ?* in formal, and *Et toi ?* in informal settings.

# Other basic expressions

Here are other basic expressions used in everyday situations that you must keep in mind.

| *Oui* | Yes |
|---|---|
| *Non* | No |
| *S'il vous plaît* | Please <br> ex. *Je voudrais une baguette, **s'il vous plaît.*** <br> (I would like a baguette, please.) |
| *Pardon* | Pardon me; Excuse me <br> ex. ***Pardon ? Pouvez-vous répéter s'il vous plaît ?*** <br> (Pardon me? Can you repeat that please?) |

| | |
|---|---|
| | When you bump into someone by accident, you can also use *pardon* to apologize. If you go to Paris, you'll hear this word a lot in crowded subway stations! |
| ***Excusez-moi*** | Excuse me<br>ex. ***Excusez-moi, où est la gare ?***<br>(Excuse me, where is the train station?) |
| ***Merci (beaucoup)*** | Thank you (very much) |

## Key Takeaways

Let's see what we learned today before moving on to the practice exercises.

- The social setting will indicate the proper greeting to use, as well as the appropriate pronoun "you" (*tu* or *vous*). We learned the difference between formal and informal situations.

| Formal Situations | Informal Situations |
|---|---|
| Talking to a stranger | Talking to family and friends |
| Addressing people in professional situations (for example, employee to boss or student to teacher) | Talking to close colleagues and classmates |
| Addressing people in commercial situations (at a shop, bank, restaurant, etc.) | Talking to a child |

- The most common ways to say "hello" are *bonjour*, *bonsoir*, *salut* and *coucou.*
- The most common ways to say "goodbye" are *au revoir*, *bonne journée*, *bonne soirée*, and *salut.*
- To ask one's name, introduce oneself, or introduce someone else, we use the verb *s'appeler*.

| Asking one's name |
|---|
| *Comment vous appelez-vous ? / Vous vous appelez comment ?* |

| |
|---|
| *Comment tu t'appelles ? / Tu t'appelles comment ?* |
| **Introducing oneself** |
| *Je m'appelle…* |
| *Moi, c'est…* |
| **Introducing someone else** |
| *Il s'appelle… / Elle s'appelle…* |
| *Ils s'appellent… / Elles s'appellent…* |
| *Voici mon ami / mes amis…* |

- French verbs are conjugated according to the pronouns. The subject pronouns are *je, tu, il, elle, nous, vous, ils* and *elles.*
- We learned how to conjugate the verb *s'appeler: je m'appelle, tu t'appelles, il/elle s'appelle, nous nous appelons, vous vous appelez, ils/elles s'appellent.*
- *Tu* and *vous* both refer to the pronoun "you". *Tu* is used when talking to family, friends, or children. *Vous* is for formal situations. It is also used when referring to two or more people.
- To ask how someone is, you can say *Comment allez-vous ?* or *Vous allez bien ?* in formal situations. In casual settings, say *Tu vas bien ?* or *Ça va ?* To respond, we use the following expressions accordingly, *Je vais bien* or *Ça va (bien).*

In the next chapter, we will learn more about introducing oneself, like indicating one's profession and age. We will also talk about two very important verbs, *être* (to be) and *avoir* (to have).

# Exercises

How about putting to use what we've learned so far? Complete the exercises below to test your understanding of this chapter.

1. Categorize the following greetings. Which ones are used to greet somebody? Which ones are used to say goodbye?

*Bonsoir • Coucou • Salut • Bonne journée •*
*Bonjour • Bonne fin de journée • À plus*

| Greetings | Parting Expressions |
|---|---|
| | |

2. Choose the appropriate response to the following sentence: *Comment allez-vous ?*

    a. Je m'appelle Fabienne.
    b. Oui, ça va.
    c. Très bien, et vous ?

3. Choose the appropriate response: *Comment tu t'appelles ?*

    a. Bien, merci.
    b. Moi, c'est Sophie.
    c. Ils s'appellent Adrien et Olivier.

4. You enter a shop in the evening. How would you greet the vendors?

    a. Bonsoir.
    b. Ça va ?
    c. Bon après-midi.

5. Complete with the correct form of *s'appeler*: Tu _____ comment?

6. Choose the appropriate response: *Comment ça va ?*

    a. À tout à l'heure.
    b. Ça va bien.
    c. Adieu.

7. Complete with the correct form of *s'appeler*: Elle_____Zoé.

8. Complete the dialogue with the appropriate word or phrase:

    - Bonjour !_____?
    - Je m'appelle Jules, et_____?
    - Moi,_____Nathan.
    - Enchanté.

9. Associate the following expressions to the correct translation:

                           See you soon

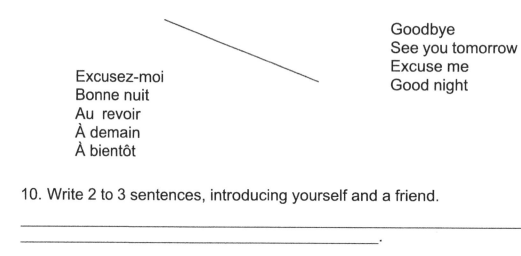

Excusez-moi
Bonne nuit
Au  revoir
À demain
À bientôt

Goodbye
See you tomorrow
Excuse me
Good night

10. Write 2 to 3 sentences, introducing yourself and a friend.

_____

_____.

_____

_____

# Answer Key

1.

| Greetings | Parting Expressions |
|---|---|
| Bonsoir | Salut |
| Coucou | Bonne journée |
| Salut | Bonne fin de journée |
| Bonjour | *À plus* |

2. c

3. b

4. a

5. t'appelles

6. b

7. s'appelle

8.　　　- Bonjour ! <u>Comment vous appelez-vous / Vous vous appelez comment</u> ?
　　　- Je m'appelle Jules, et <u>vous</u> ?
　　　- Moi, <u>c'est</u> Nathan.
　　　- Enchanté.

9.

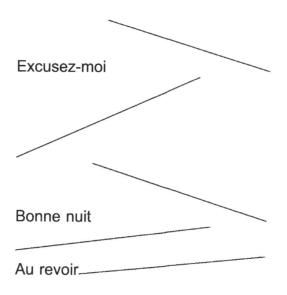

Excusez-moi

Bonne nuit

Au revoir

See you soon
Goodbye
See you tomorrow
Excuse me
Good night

À demain
À bientôt

10. Sample response: *Bonjour ! Je m'appelle Marie. Voici mon ami, Lucas.*

# Chapter 2: All about you

*Je pense, donc je suis.*

I think, therefore I am.

- René Descartes

You now know how to greet someone, introduce yourself and ask how someone is. After meeting someone a few times, you would perhaps want to know more about him or her: his or her profession, age, country of origin, and so on. This goes both ways, as you too might be encouraged to talk a bit more about yourself.

In this lesson, you will learn how to indicate and ask one's profession and age. You will also encounter *avoir* and *être*, two very important verbs at the heart of the French language. *C'est parti !* Here we go!

## Professions

Let's look at this dialogue between Pierre and Hélène.

| | |
|---|---|
| **Pierre** : *Qu'est-ce que vous faites dans la vie ?* | What do you do for a living? |
| **Hélène** : *Je suis infirmière à l'Hôpital Paris Saint-Joseph. Et vous ? Quel est votre métier ?* | I am a nurse in the Paris Saint-Joseph hospital. And you? What is your job? |
| **Pierre** : *Je suis enseignant de français à l'Université.* | I am a French teacher in the University. |

### Asking one's profession

As we learned in the previous chapter, the French language differentiates between formal and informal social settings. *Tu* is an informal "you", while *vous* is the formal variation. Keep this in mind when asking for someone's profession. In informal settings, we might ask:

> *Qu'est-ce que tu fais dans la vie ?*
> *Tu fais quoi dans la vie ?*

What do you do for a living? (lit. What do you do in life?)

That potentially alarming jumble of words *Qu'est-ce que* simply refers to the interrogative pronoun "what". The pronunciation is not complicated: /kehs-keuh/. Now, both the sentences above translate to "What do you do for a living?" *Vie* means "life", as in the famous Edith Piaf song *La vie en rose* (Life in pink).

Otherwise, you can also use the following expressions:

> *Qu'est-ce que tu fais comme métier ?*
> *Qu'est-ce que tu fais comme travail ?*

Both mean, "What do you do as a job?". The words *métier* and *travail* are synonymous, and refer to the noun "job" or "work".

In formal situations, you guessed it, we use the pronoun *vous*.

> *Qu'est-ce que vous faites dans la vie ?*
> *Qu'est-ce que vous faites comme métier ?*
> *Qu'est-ce que vous faites comme travail ?*

In even more formal settings, like an interview for a visa application for example, you might hear the expressions below:

> *Quel est votre métier ?*
> *Quelle est votre profession ?*

---

**CULTURE TIP**
*How NOT to start a French conversation*

Money, religion and politics – these are three topics you really don't want to talk about with someone you are just meeting for the first time. Don't ask how much someone makes or what is one's religion. These can be seen as intrusive questions. Asking for one's political preferences is just as risky a terrain.

---

Some things that in other cultures are natural can be seen as impolite in France. For example, asking someone's profession when you just met is not a common thing. This is because it has something to do with one of the taboo topics above: money. Asking about someone's civil status, whether one is married or has kids, can also be considered rude.

So what exactly can you talk about? Well, first-meeting conversations can revolve around culture. You can chat about French gastronomy, art or music, without worrying about causing someone discomfort!

### Indicating one's profession

To indicate one's profession in English, we use the verb "to be". For example, "I **am** a teacher." It's the same in French, where we use the verb *être*, the equivalent of "to be". Remember that French verbs are conjugated according to the subject. Here's how we conjugate the verb *être* in the present tense:

| être | | |
|---|---|---|
| **Je** | suis | /swee/ |
| **Tu** | es | /eh/ |
| **Il/Elle** | est | /eh/ |
| **Nous** | sommes | /sohm/ |
| **Vous** | êtes | /eht/ |
| **Ils/Elles** | sont | /sohN/ |

Are all verb conjugations so complicated? The verb *être* is actually an irregular verb, so don't panic. Verb conjugations are generally simpler, as we will show you later on.

Now, to indicate one's profession, we follow the same structure in English:

SUBJECT + VERB + NOUN / ADJECTIVE

For example:

**Je suis enseignant.**
I am a teacher.

So, we start with the subject *Je* (I), then add the correct conjugation of the verb *être* (am) and finally, the profession *enseignant* (teacher). Notice that in English, you would say "<u>a</u> teacher", with the indefinite article "a". In French, we omit the article, and simply say "I am teacher". Why is that? To put it simply, French professions are adjectives in this specific sentence structure. So in the example above, *enseignant* is considered an adjective, unlike in English where it is a noun.

Let's look at some other examples:

**Je suis étudiant.**
I am a student.

**Je suis médecin.**
I am a doctor.

**Je suis ingénieur.**
I am an engineer.

Since you already know all the subject pronouns and conjugated forms of *être*, you can also indicate someone else's profession or even ask a specific question. For instance:

**Elle est dentiste.**
She is a dentist.

**Ils sont boulangers**.
They are bakers.

**Nous sommes acteurs.**
We are actors.

**Vous êtes avocat ?**
Are you a lawyer? (lit. You are a lawyer?)

As we mentioned earlier, the professions in these sentence structures are adjectives. In French, adjectives change according to the gender and number of the noun. As such, professions too differ in spelling according to the subject. Look at these two examples:

*Nathan est **avocat**.*

18

Nathan is a lawyer.

*Clara est **avocate**.*
Clara is a lawyer.

Notice how the adjective *avocat* (lawyer) changes according to the subject noun. For the masculine subject, we say *avocat*, while for the feminine subject, we add an extra –e, as in *avocate*. Let's look at some more examples.

*Paul est **enseignant**.*
Paul is a teacher.

*Camille est **enseignante**.*
Camille is a teacher.

Like the word *avocat*, we add an extra –e to *enseignant* for feminine subjects.

How about plural subjects? In this case, we add an extra –s while taking into consideration the gender of the nouns. So, for instance:

*Paul et Clara sont **enseignants**.*
Paul and Clara are teachers.

*Clara et Sarah sont **enseignantes**.*
Clara and Sarah are teachers.

## *Professions vocabulary*

| Masculine form | Feminine form | Translation |
| --- | --- | --- |
| acteur | actrice | actor |
| boulanger | boulangère | baker |
| charpentier | charpentière | carpenter |
| chef | | cook |
| dentiste | | dentist |
| employé | employée | employee |
| enseignant | enseignante | teacher |
| fonctionnaire | | civil servant |
| | | |

| | | |
|---|---|---|
| infirmier | infirmière | nurse |
| ingénieur | ingénieure | engineer |
| médecin | | doctor |
| policier | policière | police officer |
| serveur | serveuse | waiter |

## GRAMMAR TIP
### Noun-adjective agreement for professions

Noun-adjective agreement simply means that French adjectives change according to the gender and number of the noun they are describing. For most adjectives, we follow two general rules:

- To form the feminine, we add an –e to the end of the masculine adjective.
- To form the plural, we add an –s.

And so, *avocat* (lawyer) would be *avocate* in feminine form. In plural form, depending on the gender of the nouns, the adjective can be *avocats* or *avocates*.

Are there exceptions? Yes, there are. There are certain adjectives that generally call for different endings or that require no change at all.

| Professions ending in | | The feminine form is… |
|---|---|---|
| -ien | → | -ienne |
| -er | → | -ère |
| -eur | → | -euse |
| -teur | → | -trice |
| -iste | → | -iste |
| -e | → | -e |

And so, *opticien* (optician) becomes *opticienne* in feminine form. *Boulanger* becomes *boulangère*; *serveur* becomes *serveuse*; *acteur* becomes *actrice*. *Pharmacien* (pharmacist) does not change in form. It is the same for adjectives already ending in –e. For example, *dentiste* is used for both masculine and feminine forms.

---

# Age and numbers

The conversation between Pierre and Hélène continues:

**Pierre** : *Vous avez quel âge ?*
How old are you?

**Hélène** : *J'ai vingt-neuf ans. Et vous ?*
I'm twenty-nine years old. And you?

**Pierre** : *J'ai trente-trois ans.*
I'm thirty-three years old.

### Asking one's age

To ask one's age in formal situations, we can say:

**Vous avez quel âge ?**
How old are you? (lit. You have what age?)

**Quel âge avez-vous ?**
How old are you? (lit. What age do you have?)

For informal settings, use the following expression:

**Tu as quel âge ?**
How old are you? (lit. You have what age?)

In the French language, age is indicated with the verb "to have". In English for instance, one would say "How old are you?" or "I am 20 years old", using the verb "to be" (are). In French however, the literal translation of these expressions are "What age do you have?" and "I have 20 years".

The verb *avoir* means "to have". It is used to indicate possession like its English counterpart. For example, you can say, *J'ai un sac* (I have a bag). *Avoir* is also used in special cases like in indicating one's age. To conjugate:

| *avoir* | | |
|---------|-----|------|
| **J'** | ai | /ay/ |

| | | |
|---|---|---|
| **Tu** | as | /ah/ |
| **Il/Elle** | a | /ah/ |
| **Nous** | avons | /ah-vohñ/ |
| **Vous** | avez | /ah-vay/ |
| **Ils/Elles** | ont | /ohñ/ |

Notice that we contract the pronoun *Je* before a vowel, so *Je ai* becomes *J'ai* (I have). This is not the universe's way to make your French learner's life more complicated. Quite the contrary, we contract *Je* to simplify the pronunciation. Isn't it much easier to say *J'ai* than *Je ai*?

### *Indicating one's age*

To say your age in French, we use the following structure:

SUBJECT + *AVOIR* + NUMBER + the word *ANS* (years).

Here are some examples:

- *J'ai 10 ans.*
- *Elle a 47 ans.*
- *Vous avez 30 ans ?*
- *Hugo a 25 ans.*

The word *ans* translates to "years". And so, the last sentence literally means "Hugo has 25 years". Of course, in order to say your age, you'd have to know how to count!

### *Numbers 1 to 50*

Take the time to memorize numbers 1 to 50 before moving forward.

| | | | | | |
|---|---|---|---|---|---|
| **0** | zéro | | | | |
| **1** | un | **21** | vingt et un | **41** | quarante et un |
| **2** | deux | **22** | vingt-deux | **42** | quarante-deux |
| **3** | trois | **23** | vingt-trois | **43** | quarante-trois |
| **4** | quatre | **24** | vingt-quatre | **44** | quarante-quatre |
| **5** | cinq | **25** | vingt-cinq | **45** | quarante-cinq |
| **6** | six | **26** | vingt-six | **46** | quarante-six |
| **7** | sept | **27** | vingt-sept | **47** | quarante-sept |

| | | | | | |
|---|---|---|---|---|---|
| 8 | huit | 28 | vingt-huit | 48 | quarante-huit |
| 9 | neuf | 29 | vingt-neuf | 49 | quarante-neuf |
| 10 | dix | 30 | trente | 50 | cinquante |
| 11 | onze | 31 | trente et un | | |
| 12 | douze | 32 | trente-deux | | |
| 13 | treize | 33 | trente-trois | | |
| 14 | quatorze | 34 | trente-quatre | | |
| 15 | quinze | 35 | trente-cinq | | |
| 16 | seize | 36 | trente-six | | |
| 17 | dix-sept | 37 | trente-sept | | |
| 18 | dix-huit | 38 | trente-huit | | |
| 19 | dix-neuf | 39 | trente-neuf | | |
| 20 | vingt | 40 | quarante | | |

From twenty onwards, you simply need to add numbers 1 to 9 to the tens (*vingt, trente, quarante…*) to form the numbers. This makes them easier to remember.

How do I memorize all this, you say? Practice is key. Try saying your telephone number aloud to practice. Or better yet, read all the phone numbers in your contacts list. Another great idea would be to use number flashcards. Want an extra challenge? Opt for addition or multiplication flashcards!

# Key Takeaways

- To ask one's profession and age, we use the following expressions:

| **Asking one's profession** |
|---|
| *Qu'est-ce que tu fais dans la vie ?* <br> *Tu fais quoi dans la vie ?* |
| *Qu'est-ce que vous faites dans la vie ?* <br> *Qu'est-ce que vous faites comme métier ?* <br> *Qu'est-ce que vous faites comme travail ?* <br> *Quel est votre métier ?* <br> *Quelle est votre profession ?* |
| **Asking one's age** |

> *Tu as quel âge ?*
> *Vous avez quel âge ?*
> *Quel âge avez-vous ?*

- To indicate one's profession, we use the verb *être: je suis, tu es, il/elle est, nous sommes, vous êtes, ils/elles sont.*
- To indicate one's age, we use the verb *avoir: j'ai, tu as, il/elle a, nous avons, vous avez, ils/elles ont.*
- French adjectives agree in gender and number with the noun they describe. Generally, we form the feminine by adding an –e to the adjective, and the plural by adding an –s.

In the next chapter, you will learn how to indicate the languages you speak, as well as your country of origin. We will also have a look at what we call – ER verbs. These are regular verbs that are much easier to conjugate than *avoir* and *être,* we promise!

## Exercises

*1.* Choose the appropriate response to the following sentence: *Qu'est-ce que vous faites comme métier ?*

  a. Je m'appelle Arthur.
  b. Je suis actrice.
  c. Vous êtes dentiste.
  d. J'ai 22 ans.

*2.* Choose the appropriate response: *Tu as quel âge ?*

  a. Il a 33 ans.
  b. J'ai 22 ans.
  c. Vous avez 41 ans.
  d. Je vais bien.

*3.* Choose the appropriate response: *Lucas a quel âge ?*

  a. Elle a 12 ans.
  b. Ils ont 22 ans.
  c. Il a 17 ans.

*4.* Choose the appropriate response: *Vous êtes enseignants ?*

    a. Oui, je suis infirmière.
    b. J'ai 12 ans.
    c. Non, nous sommes étudiants.

5 – 7. Read the following text and indicate whether the statements below are true or false.

> *Jules et Marie sont mariés. Jules a cinquante ans. Il est enseignant de mathématiques. Marie a quarante-neuf ans. Elle est médecin.*

    5. Marie is a doctor.
    6. Jules is younger than Marie.
    7. Jules teaches French.

8 – 10. Answer the following mathematical problems. Write down the answers in words, not in figures.

    8. $10 \times 3 =$ _____

    9. $50 - 23 =$ _____

    10. $8 + 3 =$ _____

# Answer Key

1. b
2. b
3. c
4. c
5. True.
6. False. Jules is 50 years old while Marie is 49.
7. False. Jules teaches Mathematics.
8. trente
9. vingt-sept
10. onze

# Chapter 3: I speak a little French

*Avoir une autre langue, c'est posséder une deuxième âme.*

To have another language is to possess a second soul.

- Charlemagne

Wouldn't it be nice to be able to say "I speak French"? Or at least, "I speak a little French"? Well, by the end of this chapter, you'll be able to say it so proudly! If you meet French natives while traveling in France, you might find yourself being asked where you're from or what other languages you speak. This chapter will also prepare you for such instances.

In this lesson, you will learn how to indicate and ask one's language, nationality and country of origin. You will also learn how to conjugate your first regular verbs and produce basic subject-predicate sentences.

## Nationalities

### Asking and indicating one's nationality

To ask one's nationality, you can say:

**Vous êtes de quelle nationalité ?**
What is your nationality? (lit. You are of what nationality?)

**Vous venez d'où ?**
Where do you come from? (lit. You come from where?)

Can you tell which verb is used in the first sentence? Yes, it's the verb *être* (to be) that we learned in the previous chapter. In more formal scenarios, you might also be asked:

**Quelle est votre nationalité ?**
What is your nationality?

Now, to answer these two questions, you use the same structure as you would in English:

SUBJECT + VERB + ADJECTIVE.

And so, for instance, you might say "I am American". In French, using the verb *être*, that would be:

**Je suis américain.**

**Je suis américaine.**

Like we've seen earlier, adjectives change according to the gender of the noun it refers to. Masculine subjects would thus say *américain*; and feminine subjects, *américaine* with an added –e. Let's look at other examples.

**Harry est anglais. Amelia est anglaise.**
Harry is English. Amelia is English.

**Mario et Alessandro sont italiens.**
Mario and Alessandro are Italian.

**Mei et Yui sont japonaises.**
Mei and Yui are Japanese.

**Mon amie Sofia est espagnole.**
My friend Sofia is Spanish.

**Nous sommes vietnamiens.**
We are Vietnamese.

In the next section, you will find a list of some nationalities, in both masculine and feminine forms.

### Nationalities vocabulary

| Masculine form | Feminine form | Translation |
|---|---|---|
| *allemand* | *allemande* | German |
| *américain* | *américaine* | American |
| *anglais* | *anglaise* | English |
| *autrichien* | *autrichienne* | Austrian |

| | | |
|---|---|---|
| *belge* | *belge* | Belgian |
| *canadien* | *canadienne* | Canadian |
| *chinois* | *chinoise* | Chinese |
| *coréen* | *coréenne* | Korean |
| *espagnol* | *espagnole* | Spanish |
| *français* | *française* | French |
| *grec* | *grecque* | Greek |
| *japonais* | *japonaise* | Japanese |
| *marocain* | *marocaine* | Moroccan |
| *mexicain* | *mexicaine* | Mexican |
| *portugais* | *portugaise* | Portuguese |
| *russe* | *russe* | Russian |
| *suédois* | *suédoise* | Swede |
| *vietnamien* | *vietnamienne* | Vietnamese |

Remember that as a general rule, we add an –e to adjectives to form the feminine, and an –s to form the plural. Notice however, that this is not the case for certain adjectives of nationality. To make it simpler, we've summarized the common rules below. We've also included pronunciation notes. The pronunciation of the feminine form may sometimes differ from the masculine form.

| Nationalities ending in... | Add... | Examples |
|---|---|---|
| -ais<br>-ois<br>-ain<br>-and<br>-ol | -e | *français → français* **e**<br>/frahñ-seh/ → /frahñ-seh **z**/ |
| | | *chinois → chinois* **e**<br>/shee-nwah/ → / shee-nwah**z**/ |
| | | *américain → américain* **e**<br>/ah-meh-ree-kahñ / →/ ah-meh-ree-**kehn**/ |
| | | *allemand → allemand* **e**<br>/ah-leh-mahñ/ → /ah-leh-mahñ **D**/ |
| | | *espagnol → espagnol* **e** |

| | | /ehs-pah-nyol/ (no change in pronunciation) |
|---|---|---|
| -ien<br>-éen | -ne | canadien → canadien **ne**<br>/kah-nah-dyahñ/ → / kah-nah-dy**eh**n/ |
| | | coréen → coréen **ne**<br>/ko-re-yahñ/ → /ko-re-y **eh**n/ |
| -e | none | russe<br>/rews/ (no change in pronunciation) |

The word for "Greek" is an irregular case. For masculine subjects, we say *grec* and for feminine, *grecque*. Both are pronounced the same way, as /grek/.

# Languages

### Asking and indicating one's language

If you want to ask which languages one speaks, you can say:

**Vous parlez quelles langues ?**
You speak which languages?

**Quelles langues parlez-vous ?**
Which languages do you speak?

The second expression is used in more formal scenarios. As you know by now, in informal situations, we use the pronoun *tu*.

**Tu parles quelles langues ?**
You speak which languages?

To indicate which languages you speak, we also use the verb *parler* (to speak). In English, one might say "I speak English". In French, that would be:

**Je parle anglais.**
I speak English.

A quick writing tip: the first letter of languages and nationalities are not capitalized in French. Let's look at some other examples:

**Mathis parle français.**
Mathis speaks French.

**Elle parle mandarin et arabe.**
She speaks Mandarin and Arabic.

**Nous parlons un peu espagnol.**
We speak a little Spanish.

**Je parle couramment italien.**
I speak Italian fluently.

As in the last two sentences, you can use *un peu* (a little) and *couramment* (fluently) to specify your fluency in the language.

---

**GRAMMAR TIP**
*-ER verbs in French*

There are three types of French regular verbs, categorized according to their endings. –ER verbs are those whose unconjugated forms end in –er. –IR verbs end in –ir while –RE verbs end in –re. And so, for example, *parler* is an –ER verb; *venir* (to come) is an –IR verb and *descendre* (to go down) is an –RE verb.

Now what's this all about, you might ask? These categorizations actually make learning verb conjugations much easier. Simply because, all verbs under the same category are usually conjugated the exact same way!

To conjugate –ER verbs in the present tense, we simply remove the –er of the infinitive form and replace them with a set of fixed endings. And so, for example, we remove the –er in the verb *parler* and then we add the appropriate endings:

---

| parler | → parl | | |
|--------|--------|--------|--------------|
| **Je** | +e | parl**e** | I speak |
| **Tu** | +es | parl**es** | You speak (inf.) |
| **Il/Elle** | +e | parl**e** | He/She speaks |
| **Nous** | +ons | parl**ons** | We speak |
| **Vous** | +ez | parl**ez** | You speak (for.) |
| **Ils/Elles** | +ent | parl**ent** | They speak |

Thus, in order to conjugate a verb within a category, all you have to do is keep in mind the endings for each pronoun.

### Languages vocabulary

You'll notice that in French, most of the languages are in fact the word for the nationalities in masculine form. And so, English would be *anglais*, French would be *français* and Russian would be *russe*. Of course, there are some languages that don't share the term with the words for nationality. For example, *mandarin* for Mandarin, *pendjabi* for Punjabi or *swahili* for Swahili.

# Cities and Countries

### Asking and indicating where you live

To ask where someone lives, use the verb *habiter*:

**Vous habitez où ?**
Where do you live?

To indicate where you live, you might specify your city and country by saying:

**J'habite à New York, aux États-Unis.**
I live in New York, in the US.

The verb *habiter* (to live) is an –ER verb because it ends with –er. It is thus in the same category as the verb *parler* and is conjugated the same way:

| habiter | → *habit* | |
|---|---|---|
| **J'** | +e | habit**e** |
| **Tu** | +es | habit**es** |
| **Il/Elle** | +e | habit**e** |
| **Nous** | +ons | habit**ons** |
| **Vous** | +ez | habit**ez** |
| **Ils/Elles** | +ent | habit**ent** |

Since the h is silent, we contract the pronoun *je* before the verb. It's just like what we saw with the verb *avoir*. And so, we say *j'habite* /jah-beet/, and not *je habite*.

Now that you understand the conjugation of the verb *habiter*, let's focus our attention on the prepositions.

Before cities, we always use the preposition *à*, which is an equivalent of "in" in English. So you might say, *à Paris, à Tokyo, à Rome, à Jakarta*, etc. For countries, the preposition changes according to gender and number.

Gender again? Yes, but we promise you'll soon get used to it. As you're probably realizing by now, gender is an important part of the French language. In French, every noun has a gender, including countries.

Let's look at how the preposition *à* (in) changes according to the gender and number of the country:

| For countries that… | Preposition à | Examples |
|---|---|---|
| are feminine | *en* | *en* France, *en* Grèce |
| start with a vowel | | *en* Iran, *en* Italie |
| are masculine | *au* | *au* Canada, *au* Japon |
| are plural | *aux* | *aux* États-unis, *aux* Philippines |

Of course, the million-dollar question is, how do you know the gender of the countries? Those ending in –e are feminine (ex. *France, Italie, Pologne, Corée*). The rest is masculine. The good news is there are only four exceptions to this rule: *Cambodge*, *Mexique*, *Zimbabwe* and *Mozambique* are masculine nouns.

It is simpler to know which countries are plural. More often than not, if they are plural in English, it's the same in French. For example, the United States (*les États-unis*), the United Arab Emirates (*les Émirats arabes unis*), or the Netherlands (*les Pays-Bas*).

### Countries vocabulary

| Masculine | | Feminine | |
|---|---|---|---|
| *le Canada* | Canada | *la Chine* | China |
| *le Danemark* | Denmark | *la Grèce* | Greece |
| *le Japon* | Japan | *la France* | France |
| *le Portugal* | Portugal | *la Pologne* | Poland |
| *le Royaume-Uni* | the United Kingdom | *la Russie* | Russia |
| **Plural** | | | |
| les *États-unis* | | the United States | |
| les *Émirats arabes unis* | | the United Arab Emirates | |
| les *Pays-Bas* | | the Netherlands | |

---

**CULTURE TIP**
*The World of Francophonie*

*La Francophonie* refers to the community of francophones or French speakers. There are currently 29 countries that speak French as a national or official language: Belgium, Benin, Burkina Faso, Burundi, Cameroon, Canada, Chad, the Ivory Coast, the Democratic Republic of the Congo, Djibouti, Equatorial Guinea, France, Haiti, Luxembourg, Madagascar, Mali, Monaco, Niger, Rwanda, Senegal, Seychelles, Switzerland, Togo and Vanuatu.

---

# Key Takeaways

- To ask and indicate one's nationality, we use the following expressions:

**Ask one's nationality**

*Vous êtes de quelle nationalité ?*
*Vous venez d'où ?*
*Quelle est votre nationalité ?*

**Indicate one's nationality**

Subject pronoun + *être* + nationality adjective

- Adjectives of nationality agree in gender and number with the noun it refers to. Generally, for nationalities ending in –ais, –ois, –ain, –and, –ol, we simply add an –e to form the feminine. For those ending in – ien or –éen, we add –ne. Nationalities that already end in –e in masculine form does not change in the feminine form. To form the plural, we add an –s.
- To ask and indicate one's language, we use the following expressions:

**Ask one's language**

*Vous parlez quelles langues ?*
*Quelles langues parlez-vous ?*
*Tu parles quelles langues ?*

**Indicate one's language**

Subject pronoun + *parler* + (*un peu/couramment*) + language

- To conjugate –ER verbs, we remove the –er ending and add the following: *-e, -es, -e, -ons, -ez, -ent*
- To ask and indicate where one lives, we use the following expressions:

**Ask where one lives**

*Vous habitez où ?*

### Indicate one's city and country

Subject pronoun + *habiter* + *à* + place

- The preposition *à* changes according to the gender and number of the country. Most countries ending in –e are feminine, and those in –s, plural.
- When referring to cities, the preposition *à* does not change.

In the next chapter, you will learn how to present and describe common objects using the expressions *c'est* and *ce sont*. We will also look at some basic French adjectives.

## Exercises

*1.* Answer the question using the expressions learned: *Vous êtes de quelle nationalité ?*

*2.* Answer the question using the expressions learned: *Vous parlez quelles langues ?*

*3 – 7.* What is the feminine form of the following nationalities?

3. français → _____
4. coréen → _____
5. italien → _____
6. grec → _____
7. russe → _____

8-10. Complete the text with the correct form of the preposition *à*.

*Bonjour ! Je m'appelle Sandrine. Je suis française, mais j'habite actuellement 8.____ Tokyo, 9.____ Japon. Voici mon amie Mei. Elle est chinoise. Elle parle couramment anglais. Elle habite à Beijing, 10. Chine.*

# Answer Key

1. Sample answer: Je suis américain.
2. Sample answer: Je parle anglais, espagnol et un peu français.
3. française
4. coréenne
5. italienne
6. grecque
7. russe
8. à
9. au
10. en

# Chapter 4: This is not a pipe

*Ceci n'est pas une pipe.*

This is not a pipe.

- René Magritte

Do you know Belgian surrealist painter René Magritte? Our title comes from his painting called *La Trahison des Images* (The Treachery of Images). It is a painting of a pipe with the inscription *Ceci n'est pas une pipe* (This is not a pipe). It simply means that the pipe in the painting is not a pipe, but the painting of a pipe! Phew!

In this lesson, we will learn how to present and describe something. We won't use *ceci* like Magritte, for this is actually a formal term for the pronoun "this". Instead, we'll focus on more natural sounding expressions like *c'est* and *ce sont*. Alongside, we will also learn about articles and adjectives in this chapter.

## Presenting something

### C'est and ce sont

To present something or someone, we use the expressions *c'est* and *ce sont*. *Ce* or the contracted *C'* is the equivalent of the demonstrative pronouns "this" and "these". As you can see, they are combined with the verb *être*. *C'est* means "this is" or "it is". *Ce sont* translates to "these are" or "they are". You can combine these expressions with a noun, a pronoun, an adjective or an adverb. Let's look at some examples:

**C'est un livre.**
It's a book. / This is a book.

**Ce sont des livres.**
These are books.

**C'est moi.**
It's me.

**C'est facile.**
It's easy.
**C'est bientôt.**
It's soon.

For now, let us focus on the first two sentences above. Notice how we use *C'est* for singular nouns (*un livre*), and *Ce sont* for plural nouns (*des livres*). Observe these other examples:

**C'est un sac. Ce sont des sacs.**
This is a bag. These are bags.

**C'est une photo. Ce sont des photos.**
This is a photo. These are photos.

Remember that you will choose between these two expressions according to the number of the noun referred to.

---

## GRAMMAR TIP
### *Definite and indefinite articles*

There are two types of articles in French: definite and indefinite. Definite articles refer to the word "the" in English, while indefinite articles are the equivalent of "a" and "an". For example:

*C'est **un** livre.* (It's a book.)
*C'est **le** livre que j'adore.* (It's the book I love.)

Like in English, you use definite articles to point to a specific noun, and indefinite articles to an unspecific noun.

Now, in French, the articles change according to the gender and number of the noun. In English, there is only one "the", in French there are four. In English, we have "a" and "an", while in French we have three equivalents.

In the table below, you'll find which article to use in which case. We also added some examples:

| | Indefinite articles | Definite articles |
|---|---|---|
| masculine | *un* stylo (a pen) | *le* livre (the book) |
| feminine | *une* banane (a banana) | *la* femme (the woman) |
| plural | *des* cahiers (notebooks) | *les* plantes (the plants) |
| before a vowel or *h* | | *l'*étudiant (the student) *l'*homme (the man) |

Here we go again with gender! How do you know the gender of nouns? We'll give you the abridged version of the general rule for now: Words ending in –e or –ion are often feminine, except those ending in –age, –ege, –é, or –isme, which are often masculine.

This is not a foolproof rule. In fact, we recommend that instead of memorizing the common endings, you should instead just memorize the gender of words progressively. How? Every time you come across a new word, memorize it with the article. For example, don't just memorize *livre* for book, but *un livre*, with the article indicating it is masculine.

### Common Objects Vocabulary

| | Translation |
|---|---|
| *un cahier* | a notebook |
| *un crayon* | a pencil |
| *un livre* | a book |
| *un ordinateur* | a computer |
| *un ordinateur portable* | a laptop |
| *un (téléphone) portable* | a mobile phone |
| *un sac* | a bag |
| *un sac à dos* | a backpack |
| *un stylo* | a pen |
| *un tableau blanc* | a whiteboard |
| *une chaise* | a chair |

| | |
|---|---|
| *une règle* | a ruler |
| *une table* | a table |

**CULTURE TIP**
*20 for God*

French schools and universities use a 20-point grading system with 20 being the highest. But there is a common saying that goes: "20 is for God, 19 is for the King and 18 is for the President." And so, the highest score students would often get is a 17. In reality, a grade of 14 is already considered good!

If you study in France, you will receive your diploma with the specification of your *mention* or honors. A grade of 14 to 16 yields a *mention bien* (good), 16 to 18 a *mention très bien* (very good) and 18 above a *mention excellent* (outstanding).

# Describing something

Using the expressions *c'est* and *ce sont*, you can also describe something:

*C'est **délicieux** !*
It's delicious. / This is delicious.

*C'est **difficile**.*
It's difficult.

Or you can also use it with a noun and adjective combination:

*C'est un stylo **noir**.*

It's a black pen.

*C'est une femme **gentille**.*
It's a kind woman.

*C'est une **petite** maison.*
It's a small house.

## Common Adjectives Vocabulary

| Adjectives | Translation |
|---|---|
| *beau (m.) / belle (f.)* | beautiful |
| *blanc (m.) / blanche (f.)* | white |
| *bon marché (m./f.)* | cheap |
| *cher (m.) / chère (f.)* | expensive |
| *court (m.) / courte (f.)* | short |
| *difficile (m./f.)* | difficult |
| *facile (m./f.)* | easy |
| *faible (m./f.)* | weak |
| *fort (m.) / forte (f.)* | strong |
| *gentil (m.) / gentille (f.)* | kind |
| *grand (m.) / grande (f.)* | big |
| *heureux (m.) / heureuse (f.)* | happy |
| *laid (m.) / laide (f.)* | ugly |
| *léger (m.) / légère (f.)* | light |
| *long (m.) / longue (f.)* | long |
| *lourd (m.) / lourde (f.)* | heavy |
| *petit (m.) / petite (f.)* | small |
| *triste (m./f.)* | sad |
| *méchant (m.) / méchante (f.)* | mean |
| *noir (m.) / noire (f.)* | black |

## Placing adjectives

In French, adjectives are generally placed after the noun. Adjectives of color always come after the noun. For example:

*C'est un test **difficile**.*
It's a difficult test.

*C'est une chemise **blanche**.*
It's a white blouse.

Exceptions include shorter adjectives like *beau*, *bon*, *long, petit*, which are placed before the noun.

*C'est une **petite** maison.*
It's a small house.

*C'est un **long** chemin.*
It's a long road.

We will learn later on as well that certain adjectives change meaning according to their position. But let's not get ahead of ourselves! For now, remember these two rules.

## Key Takeaways

- To present or describe something, we use the expressions *C'est* (It is / This is) and *Ce sont* (They are / These are). These two can be followed by a noun, pronoun, an adjective or an adverb.
- The definite articles in French are: *le* (m.), *la* (f.), *les* (plur.) and *l'* (before a vowel). All of these translate to "the" in English.
- The indefinite articles in French are: *un* (m.), *une* (f.) and *des* (pl.). All of these translate to "a" or "an" in English.
- Nouns ending in –e or –ion are often feminine, except those ending in –age, –ege, –é, or –isme, which are often masculine.
- Adjectives in French are usually placed after the noun. Certain shorter adjectives such as *beau, bon, long, petit* are placed before the noun.

In the next chapter, you will learn how to ask for information politely. You will also learn how to say numbers above 50 and how to read telephone numbers in French.

# Exercises

1-5. Present the following objects using *c'est* or *ce sont*:

    1. A book
    2. A pen
    3. Some photos
    4. A black notebook
    5. Some heavy bags

*6.* Complete with the correct <u>indefinite</u> article: *Ce sont_____ordinateurs.*

*7.* Complete with the correct <u>definite</u> article: *C'est_____chaise blanche.*

*8.* Complete with the correct <u>indefinite</u> article: *C'est_____homme méchant.*

9. Add the correct form of the adjective "kind": *C'est une femme.*

10. Add the correct form of the adjective "small": *C'est une table.*

# Answer Key

1. C'est un livre.
2. C'est un stylo.
3. Ce sont des photos.
4. C'est un cahier noir.
5. Ce sont des sacs lourds.
6. des
7. la
8. un
9. C'est une femme <u>gentille</u>.
10. C'est une <u>petite</u> table.

# Chapter 5: How may I help you?

*Un peu d'aide nous fait grand bien.*

A little help does us a lot of good.

\- Jean Frain du Tremblay

If traveling or moving to France, it is essential to know how to ask and gather information. By learning how to formulate questions, you will be able to get by in various instances, as in asking for help at the train station, post office or bank.

In this lesson, you will learn how to obtain information using the interrogative pronoun *quel* and the conditional expression *je voudrais*. We will also study the rest of the numbers in French.

## Asking for information

Isabella goes to Paris to learn French. To complete her immersion experience, she decides to enroll in a language course. She asks for information at the reception:

**Receptionist**: *Bonjour, comment puis-je vous aider ?*
**Isabella**: *Bonjour Madame. C'est pour une inscription. Je voudrais des informations s'il vous plaît.*
**Receptionist**: *Bien sûr. C'est pour quelle langue ?*
**Isabella**: *Le français pour débutants.*
**Receptionist**: *D'accord. Vous complétez un formulaire et vous présentez une pièce d'identité…*
**Isabella**: *Et combien ça coûte ?*
**Receptionist**: *Ça coûte 400 euros pour 36 heures de cours.*

Let us focus on the expression pairs we see in the dialogue:

**Comment puis-je vous aider ?** (for.)

How may I help you?

To ask for information, we reply with:

**Je voudrais des informations s'il vous plaît.**
I would like some information please.

The polite expression *je voudrais* translates to "I would like" and is used not only when you seek information, but also when ordering in a restaurant. Note that you can specify what kind of information you are looking for with the expression *c'est*. For example: *C'est pour une inscription* (It's for an enrollment).

### Asking for price

To ask for the price, we can say:

**Combien ça coûte ?**
How much does it cost?

And to indicate the price:

**Ça coûte…**
It costs…

### Interrogative pronoun quel

The receptionist helps Isabella fill in the enrollment form. With our previous lessons, you will be able to understand most of the dialogue below:

**Receptionist:** *Quel est votre nom ?*
**Isabella:** *Bianchi.*
**Receptionist:** *Quel est votre prénom ?*
**Isabella:** *Isabella.*
**Receptionist:** *Quelle est votre nationalité ?*
**Isabella :** *Je suis italienne.*
**Receptionist:** *Quelle est votre adresse ?*
**Isabella :** *J'habite 8 avenue Émile-Zola, dans le 15ème.*
**Receptionist:** *Et quel est votre numéro de téléphone ?*

**Isabella :** *C'est le 07 64 82 30 10.*

One of the ways we can formulate a question in French is by using the interrogative pronoun *quel*. *Quel* may be roughly translated to "what" or "which". It changes according to the gender and number of the noun it refers to. For example:

**Quel (m.)** *est votre* **nom (m.) ?**
What is your surname?

**Quelle (f.)** *est votre* **nationalité (f.) ?**
What is your nationality?

Since *nom* is a masculine noun, we use *quel*; *nationalité* is a feminine noun, so we use *quelle*. The table below summarizes the variations of *quel*. All of them are pronounced the same way as /kel/.

| Gender / Number | *Quel* | Examples |
|---|---|---|
| masculine | *quel* | **Quel** *est votre nom ?* <br> **Quel** *est votre prénom ?* |
| feminine | *quelle* | **Quelle** *est votre nationalité ?* <br> **Quelle** *est votre adresse ?* |
| plural masculine | *quels* | **Quels** *sont vos noms ?* |
| plural feminine | *quelles* | **Quelles** *sont vos coordonnées ?* |

A few notes regarding the vocabulary here: *un nom* is used to refer to both surname and complete name while *un prénom* refers to one's first name. *Les coordonnées* (f. plur.) translates to "contact details". If asked for your *coordonnées*, you are thus expected to specify your address and phone number.

**GRAMMAR TIP**
*The possessive pronoun "your"*

French possessive pronouns are used much like their English counterparts. They are placed before a noun to indicate possession, for example *mon* sac (**my** bag). The only difference is that pronouns in French change according to the gender and number of the noun, not the possessor. For now, let's learn the equivalent of the pronoun *your*:

| | your (for.) |
|---|---|
| masculine | *votre* nom |
| feminine | *votre* adresse |
| plural | *vos* amis |

Note that this is the formal "your". Later on, we will learn the informal variation.

## Numbers 60 to 100

In Chapter 2, we learned numbers 1 to 50. Don't hesitate to review this chapter if needed. When you're ready, complete your vocabulary by memorizing the numbers below:

| 50 | cinquante | 70 | soixante-dix | 90 | quatre-vingt-dix |
|---|---|---|---|---|---|
| 51 | cinquante et un | 71 | soixante-et-onze | 91 | quatre-vingt-onze |
| 52 | cinquante-deux | 72 | soixante-douze | 92 | quatre-vingt-douze |
| 53 | cinquante-trois | 73 | soixante-treize | 93 | quatre-vingt-treize |
| 54 | cinquante-quatre | 74 | soixante-quatorze | 94 | quatre-vingt-quatorze |
| 55 | cinquante-cinq | 75 | soixante-quinze | 95 | quatre-vingt-quinze |
| 56 | cinquante-six | 76 | soixante-seize | 96 | quatre-vingt-seize |
| 57 | cinquante-sept | 77 | soixante-dix-sept | 97 | quatre-vingt-dix-sept |
| 58 | cinquante-huit | 78 | soixante-dix-huit | 98 | quatre-vingt-dix-huit |
| 59 | cinquante-neuf | 79 | soixante-dix-neuf | 99 | quatre-vingt-dix-neuf |
| 60 | soixante | 80 | quatre-vingts | 100 | cent |

| | | | |
|---|---|---|---|
| **61** | soixante et un | **81** | quatre-vingt-un |
| **62** | soixante-deux | **82** | quatre-vingt-deux |
| **63** | soixante-trois | **83** | quatre-vingt-trois |
| **64** | soixante-quatre | **84** | quatre-vingt-quatre |
| **65** | soixante-cinq | **85** | quatre-vingt-cinq |
| **66** | soixante-six | **86** | quatre-vingt-six |
| **67** | soixante-sept | **87** | quatre-vingt-sept |
| **68** | soixante-huit | **88** | quatre-vingt-huit |
| **69** | soixante-neuf | **89** | quatre-vingt-neuf |

---

### CULTURE TIP
**What's your number?**
French numbers are recited and written in tens. For instance, to read this mobile number:

06 89 41 22 30

***zéro six, quatre-vingt-neuf, quarante et un, vingt-deux, trente***

To give your mobile number, you will use *C'est* with the definite article *le*. This is a fixed expression, so *le* never changes.

***C'est le*** *06 89 41 22 30.*

How about practicing by reciting your own number aloud?

---

# Key Takeaways

- We learned the following expressions:

**Help or ask for information**

*Comment puis-je vous aider ?*
*Je voudrais des informations s'il vous plaît.*

*Combien ça coûte ?*
*Ça coûte…*

- To formulate questions in French, we can use the interrogative pronoun *quel*, which changes according to the gender and number of the noun it refers to: *quel* (m.), *quelle* (f.), *quels* (m.plur.), *quelles* (f.plur.).
- The possessive pronoun "your" changes according to the number of the antecedent as well: *votre* (sing.) and *vos* (pl.).
- To indicate a mobile or fixed phone number, we use the expression *C'est le*.

In the next chapter, you will learn how to present your family. We will review the verb *avoir* and learn more about possessive adjectives.

# Exercises

1-2. Complete the dialogue with the appropriate missing words:

- Bonjour Madame, comment 1._____vous aider ?
- Bonjour. C'est pour une inscription. Je 2._____ des informations s'il vous plaît.

3-4. Complete the dialogue with the appropriate missing words:

- 3._____coûte l'inscription ?
- Ça 4._____200 euros.

5. Complete with the correct form of *quel*:_____est votre prénom ?

6. Complete with the correct form of *quel*:_____sont vos coordonnées ?

7. Complete with the correct form of *quel*:_____est votre adresse ?

8. Complete with the correct form of "your": *Quelle est_____nationalité ?*

9. Complete with the correct form of "your": *Quels sont_____noms ?*

10. Write the following mobile number in letters, then read aloud: 07 12 99 56 87.

# Answer Key

1. puis-je
2. voudrais
3. Combien
4. coûte
5. Quel
6. Quelles
7. Quelle
8. votre
9. vos
10. zéro sept, douze, quatre-vingt-dix-neuf, cinquante-six, quatre-vingt-sept

# Chapter 6: One big happy family

*La famille sera toujours la base des sociétés.*

The family will always be the basis of societies.

- Honoré de Balzac

To have a beginners' fluency in French means to be able to talk about what is most intimate to you. And what topic is more intimate than family or *la famille*. In this lesson, you will learn how to present your family using possessive adjectives. We will revisit the verb *avoir* (to have) and look at vocabulary related to family.

## Talking about one's family

### Family vocabulary

We included below some terms used for informal direct address. In English, it's odd to directly address your mother as "mother". Instead, we opt for terms like "mom" or "mama". It's the same in French. One would call his or her mom, *maman* and not *mère*.

|  | Translation |
| --- | --- |
| *des frères et sœurs* | siblings |
| *un cousin* | a male cousin |
| *un enfant* | a child |
| *un fils* | a son |
| *un frère* | a brother |
| *un grand-père* | a grandfather (*papi* or *papy* for informal direct address) |

| | |
|---|---|
| *un mari* | a husband |
| *un oncle* | an uncle |
| *un parent* | a relative, a parent |
| *un père* | a father (*papa* for informal direct address) |
| *un petit-fils* | a grandson |
| *une cousine* | a female cousin |
| *une famille* | a family |
| *une femme* | a wife |
| *une fille* | a daughter |
| *une grand-mère* | a grandmother (*mamie* for informal direct address) |
| *une mère* | a mother (*maman* for informal direct address) |
| *une petite-fille* | a granddaughter |
| *une sœur* | a sister |
| *une tante* | a aunt |
| *une nièce* | a niece |
| *un neveu* | a nephew |

Can you guess the plural forms of the nouns above? Yes, we simply add the letter –s as ending! So *un père* would be *des pères*, *une cousine* becomes *des cousines*, etc. The only exceptions here are *un fils* whose plural form is also *des fils* and *un neveu*, whose plural form is *des neveux*.

### Presenting one's family

We learned in Chapter 1 how to formally present someone with the word *voici*:

> **Voici** *mes parents Sarah et Théo.*
> These are my parents, Sarah and Théo.

You can also use other formal phrases to present a family member:

> **Je vous présente** *mon mari, Jacques.*
> I present to you my husband, Jacques.

It sounds like you're presenting royalty, right? Use this expression in formal events or when talking to elders or those in positions of authority. In less formal situations, you might say:

**Je te présente** *ma femme, Louise.*
I present to you my wife, Louise.

Among friends, you'd want to use the expression *c'est* or *ce sont*:

**C'est** *mon cousin, Yanis.*
This is my cousin, Yanis.

**Ce sont** *mes parents, Emma et Jules.*
These are my parents, Emma and Jules.

At some point, conversing in French, you might also be asked how many siblings you have. Note that in French, there is no one word for siblings. Instead we use the term *des frères et sœurs* (lit. brothers and sisters):

**Vous avez combien de frères et sœurs ? (for.)**
**Tu as combien de frères et sœurs ? (inf.)**
How many siblings do you have?

Does the word *combien* look familiar? A gold star for you if you remember that we learned it in the last chapter! *Combien ça coûte* means "how much does it cost". The word *combien* is a quantity interrogative pronoun that can be roughly translated to "how much" or "how many". Let's look at other examples:

**Tu as combien de cousins ?**
How many cousins do you have?

**Vous avez combien d'enfants ?**
How many children do you have?

Note that after *combien*, the preposition *de* is never plural. However, it contracts before a vowel and becomes *d'*. This might seem like an anomaly because in English there is no preposition used after "how many". In French though, *combien* always comes with *de* when followed by a noun. In a sense, it means, "how many of something". Look at the difference between the two sentences below:

**Combien coûte** *le billet ?*

How much does the ticket cost?

*Tu as **combien de voitures** ?*
How many cars do you have?

In the first example, *combien* is followed by the verb *coûter* (to cost). In the second, it is followed by the noun *voitures*, hence we add the preposition *de*.

To specify the number of family members one has, we use the verb *avoir*. Here are some examples:

- *J'ai deux frères et trois sœurs.*
- *J'ai un enfant.*
- *Nous avons quatre enfants.*
- *Anne a douze cousins !*

## Possessive adjectives

We learned the equivalent of "your" in the previous chapter, *votre* and *vos*. It is important to remember that in French, possessive adjectives agree with the gender and number of the <u>noun referred to</u> and not the possessor. In English, one might say:

This is **his** car.

We choose "his", because we are referring to the male owner of the car. If the owner is female, we'll say:

This is **her** car.

In French, we would say:

*C'est **sa** voiture.*

The possessive adjective *sa* here can both mean "his" or "her". It has nothing to do with the gender of the possessor. But it has everything to do with the gender and number of the object possessed, *la voiture* which is a singular feminine noun.

*Ce sont **ses** voitures.*

This means "These are his/her cars". We use *ses* because this time, the object is plural.

Try translating this sentence: "This is her bag."

Remember that bag is a masculine noun in French, *un sac*. Again, we would disregard the gender of the possessor. So it would be: *C'est son sac.*

Below is a list of all the possessive adjectives in French:

| Masc. singular | Fem. singular | Plural | Translation |
|---|---|---|---|
| mon | ma<br>mon (before a vowel) | mes | my |
| ton | ta<br>ton (before a vowel) | tes | your (inf.) |
| son | sa<br>son (before a vowel) | ses | his / her / its |
| notre | notre | nos | our |
| votre | votre | vos | your (for.) |
| leur | leur | leurs | their |

Note that if a feminine noun starts with a vowel, we will use the adjectives *mon*, *ton*, and *son*. Why? To make pronunciation easier. For example, "my address" would be *mon adresse*, even though *adresse* is feminine, simply because it's difficult to say *ma adresse*!

**CULTURE TIP**
*Yes, I do.*

In France, there are two main forms of union that can legally bind a couple. There is of course, the traditional marriage or *le mariage*. In 1999, the government created the *PACS* or *le Pacte Civil de Solidarité* (Civil Solidarity Pact), originally as a form of union for same-sex couples. Nowadays, many straight couples choose to get *PACSÉ* instead of getting married. While it does not provide the same legal rights as a marriage, it is much easier to dissolve. Couples do not have to go through a divorce, but simply have to send a letter to the court.

The law also recognizes *le concubinage*, and no, this does not mean having a concubine! It simply means that a couple is living together but is not bound by the same obligations as a marriage or a *PACS*.

To indicate your marital status, you use the verb *être*. For example, you can say:

- *Je suis célibataire.* I am single.
- *Je suis marié(e).* I am married.
- *Je suis divorcé(e).* I am divorced.
- *Je suis pacsé(e).* I am in a civil union.

## Key Takeaways

- To present your family, you can use the following expressions: *Voici, Je vous présente, Je te présente, C'est* and *Ce sont*.
- To ask how many family members one has, we can use the expression *combien de*, which means "how many". The interrogative pronoun *combien* is combined with *de* only when followed by a noun.
- The possessive adjectives in the first person *je* are: *mon, ma* and *mes*.
- In the second person *tu* and *vous*: *ton, ta* and *tes; votre* and *vos*.
- In the first person *nous*: *notre* and *nos*.
- In the third person *il* and *elle*: *son, sa* and *ses*.
- Finally, in the third person plural *ils* and *elles*: *leur* and *leurs*.
- Possessive pronouns change in gender and number according to the noun it refers to and not according to that of the possessor.

In the next chapter, you will learn how to talk about your home and city. We will also study the prepositions of place.

## Exercises

1. Complete the dialogue with the appropriate missing words:

   - Vous avez_____enfants ?

- J'ai trois enfants : deux filles et un fils.

2. Complete the dialogue with the appropriate missing words:

- Bonjour, je vous _____ ma femme : Elle s'appelle Camille.
- Enchanté Camille.

3-6. Read the following text. Are the statements that follow true or false?

*Jacques et Camille sont mariés. Ils ont quatre enfants : Sarah, Arthur, Hugo et Nathan. Sarah, Arthur et Hugo sont célibataires. Nathan est pacsé. Il a une fille. Elle s'appelle Nathalie.*

3. Camille est la femme de Jacques.
4. Arthur est le frère de Sarah.
5. Nathan a deux enfants.
6. Jacques est le père de Nathalie.

7-10. Complete the following sentences with the correct possessive adjective, by looking at the indicated subject in the first sentence.

7. Arthur a une voiture. C'est _____ voiture.
8. Tom et Inès ont des livres. Ce sont_____livres.
9. Vous avez un enfant. C'est_____enfant.
10. J'ai une amie. C'est_____amie.

# Answer Key

1. combien d'
2. présente
3. True.
4. True.
5. False. Nathan has only one daughter.
6. False. Nathan is the father of Nathalie.
7. sa
8. leurs
9. votre
10. mon

# Chapter 7: A city dweller

*Comme une mère, une ville natale ne se remplace pas.*

Like a mother, a hometown cannot be replaced.

- Albert Memmi

Knowing the names of places in a city is not only useful for when you travel to France. It also comes in handy when you want to talk about where you come from, your hometown, what you love (or don't particularly love?) about living there.

In this lesson, you will learn how to describe your home and your city. You will also learn how to indicate the location of a place using commonly used prepositions. Are you ready to talk about *chez toi*, your home? Let's get to it!

## Talking about one's hometown

### Birthplace

In Chapter 3, we learned the expression *Vous habitez où ?*, to ask where one comes from. To this, we can reply with the phrase *J'habite à*, followed by one's city and country.

An alternative way to ask about someone's hometown is by using the verb *naître* (to be born). For example,

> ***Vous êtes né(e) où ?***
> Where were you born?

To reply, we might say,

> ***Je suis né(e) à Tokyo.***
> I was born in Tokyo.

Note that when the person referred to is female, *né* is spelled with an extra –e. But both *né* and *née* are pronounced the same way, as /nay/. *Né* is the past participle of the verb *naître*. We will learn about the past tense later on. For now, memorize this fixed expression. Take note as well of the prepositions used with countries. We learned them in Chapter 3 (*en, au, aux*).

### Places in the city vocabulary

| | Translation |
| --- | --- |
| *en ville* | in the city |
| *le centre-ville* | downtown |
| *un appartement* | an apartment |
| *un bâtiment* | a building |
| *un bureau de poste* | a post office (colloquially, one would simply say *la poste*) |
| *un café* | a coffee shop |
| *un centre commercial* | a shopping mall |
| *un cinéma* | a cinema |
| *un hôpital* | a hospital |
| *un hôtel* | a hotel |
| *un marché* | a market |
| *un musée* | a museum |
| *un parc* | a park |
| *un parking* | a parking |
| *un restaurant* | a restaurant |
| *un supermarché* | a supermarket |
| *un théâtre* | a theater |
| *une banque* | a bank |
| *une bibliothèque* | a library |
| *une école* | a school |
| *une gare* | a train station |
| *une mairie* | a city hall or town hall |

| | |
|---|---|
| une station de métro | a subway station |
| une université | a university |

Let's look at the text below. Pierre is describing his city, Paris:

*J'habite dans un appartement à Paris. Dans ma ville, il y a un cinéma, un centre commercial, des musées, des théâtres, des restaurants… Il y a tout ! Mon appartement est à côté du restaurant Chez Jean et près de la station de métro. C'est loin de l'Université où je travaille, mais le loyer n'est pas cher.*

I live in an apartment in Paris. In my city, there is a cinema, a mall, museums, theaters, restaurants… There is everything! My apartment is beside the Chez Jean restaurant and near the subway station. It is far from the University where I work, but the rent is not expensive.

To indicate places in your city, you can use *il y a*, which means "there is" or "there are". Note that *il y a* does <u>not</u> change according to the number of the noun that follows. Let's look at some examples:

*Dans ma ville, **il y a** une bibliothèque.*
In my city, there is a library.
*À Paris, **il y a** des hôtels et des restaurants partout !*
In Paris, there are hotels and restaurants everywhere!

*Dans ma ville, **il n'y a pas de** parcs.*
In my city, there are no parks.

Notice how we use *il n'y a pas de* to mean "There is no" or "there are no". Again, this is a fixed phrase that does not change according to the number of the noun.

### Prepositions of place

To specify the location of a place, we use the following prepositions:

| | Translation |
|---|---|
| *dans* | in, inside |

| | |
|---|---|
| *près de* | near |
| *loin de* | far from |
| *devant* | in front of |
| *derrière* | behind |
| *en face de* | across |
| *à côté de* | beside |
| *sur* | on, on top of |
| *sous* | under |
| *à gauche de* | to the left of |
| *à droite de* | to the right of |

Using these prepositions may be a bit challenging because they often differ from their English counterparts in terms of structure. Let's break them down, starting with the simplest ones:

*Il y a un café **dans** le musée.*
There is a coffee shop in the museum.

*Il y a un café **devant** le musée.*
There is a coffee shop in front of the museum.

*Il y a un café **derrière** le musée.*
There is a coffee shop behind the museum.

In example 1, the coffee shop is found quite literally inside the museum, *dans le musée*. Note in example 2, that *devant* is not followed by a preposition unlike the English "in front of". All of the prepositions above are simply followed by an article, in this case *le*.

On the other hand, some require the preposition *de*:

*Le restaurant est **près de l'**université.*
The restaurant is near the university.

*L'école est **loin des** parcs.*
The school is far from the parks.

*L'hôtel est **en face de la** gare.*

The hotel is across the train station.

*L'hôpital est **à côté du** parc.*
The hospital is beside the park.

*Le centre commercial est **à gauche de la** mairie.*
The mall is to the left of the city hall.

*Le cinéma est **à droite de la** poste.*
The cinema is to the right of the post office.

The preposition *de* changes according to the gender and number of the noun. Here is a table that summarizes the four variations of *de*:

| For nouns that... | Preposition *de* | Examples |
|---|---|---|
| start with a vowel | *de l'* | ***de l'**école* |
| are masculine | *du* | ***du** musée* |
| are feminine | *de la* | ***de la** mairie* |
| are plural | *des* | ***des** écoles, **des** musées* |

# Talking about one's home

In French slang, it is common to refer to one's home as *chez moi* (my place). To talk about the rooms in a house or an apartment, we use the expression *il y a*. For example:

*Dans notre appartement, **il y a** un salon, deux chambres, un bureau…*
In our apartment, there is a living room, two bedrooms, an office…

Try describing where you live. *Il y a combien de pièces ?* How many rooms are there? To help you out, we listed some common parts of the house below.

*Parts of the house vocabulary*

| | Translation |
|---|---|
| *un balcon* | a balcony |
| *un bureau* | an office |
| *un escalier* | a staircase |

| | |
|---|---|
| *un garage* | a garage |
| *un salon* | a living room |
| *un sous-sol* | a basement |
| *des w.c.* (m.plur.)<br>*des toilettes* (f.plur.) | toilets (*w.c.* is pronounced as /vay-say/) |
| *une chambre* | a bedroom |
| *une cuisine* | a kitchen |
| *une maison* | a house |
| *une pièce* | a room |
| *une salle de bain* | a bathroom |
| *une terrasse* | a patio |

## CULTURE TIP
### *Which floor again?*

You rented an apartment in France. Everything is great. The landlord tells you it is located on the second floor. You go up the stairs, but your apartment is not there! Let's imagine another situation. Imagine a building that has 3 levels. Someone who lives in America will say that the building has three floors. A French native, however, would say there are two! Are the French counting differently? You start to wonder.

Yes, they are. In France, the first floor is not the first but the zero floor. Imagine the building with three levels again. In France, the first level is called the *rez-de-chaussée* (ground floor). The second level would be the first floor (*premier étage*) and the third level would be the (*deuxième étage*). Don't get confused ever again!

Speaking of levels, to form the ordinal numbers in French, we add –ième to the number. The only exception is the word for "first", *premier* or *première*. So that would be *premier/première, deuxième, troisième… dixième, onzième*, and so on.

# Key Takeaways

- To ask where one is born, we say: *Vous êtes né(e) où ?*
- To indicate where one is born, we say: *Je suis né(e)* + preposition *à* + place.
- To indicate the existence of something, we use the expression *il y a* (there is / there are).
- The negated form of *il y a* is *il n'y a pas de* (there is no / there are no).
- The prepositions of place *dans*, *devant*, *derrière*, *sur* and *sous*, are always followed by an indefinite or a definite article.
- The prepositions *près de*, *loin de*, *en face de*, *à côté de*, *à gauche de* and *à droite de*, always require *de*.
- The preposition *de* changes according to the gender and number of the noun, or its first letter: *de l'* (before a vowel), *du* (m.), *de la* (f.), *des* (plur.).
- French ordinal numbers are formed by adding –ième to the number. The word "first", *premier* (m.) or *première* (f.), is an exception.

In the next chapter, you will learn how to talk about your hobbies. We will also look at tonic pronouns and two verbs, *faire* (to do) and *jouer* (to play).

# Exercises

*1.* Answer the following question using the expressions learned: *Vous êtes né(e) où ?*

2-5. Read the following text. Are the statements that follow true or false?

> **Pierre**: *Dans ma ville, il y a un cinéma, un centre commercial, un restaurant… mais il n'y a pas de bibliothèques. Mon appartement est à côté du bureau de poste et près de la banque. C'est très pratique.*

2. In Pierre's city, there are no libraries.
3. Pierre's apartment is far from the bank.
4. There is a shopping mall in Pierre's city.
5. Pierre's apartment is behind the post office.

6-8. Complete the sentences with the correct form of the preposition *de*.

6. La gare est loin_____université.
7. Le cinéma est à gauche_____café.
8. Le parking est en face_____restaurants.

9-10. Read the description and indicate the corresponding room in French.

9. It is the room where one sleeps.
10. It is the room where one welcomes guests.

# Answer Key

1. Sample answer: Je suis né(e) aux États-Unis OR Je suis né(e) à New York.
2. True.
3. False. It is near the bank.
4. True.
5. False. It is beside the post office.
6. de l'
7. du
8. des
9. Une chambre OR la chambre.
10. Un salon OR le salon.

# Chapter 8: The ball's in your court!

*Le loisir, voilà la plus grande joie et la plus belle conquête de l'homme.*

Leisure, this is the greatest joy and the most beautiful conquest of man.

- Rémy de Gourmont

Friendships are often formed on the basis of a shared pastime. What better way to make friends with French speakers than to share your hobbies or your likes and dislikes?

In this lesson, we will learn how to talk about leisure activities, such as music or sports. To be able to do so, you will need to study two verbs, *faire* (to do) and *jouer* (to play). We will also look at verb negation and tonic pronouns.

## Talking about one's likes and dislikes

To ask about someone's hobbies, you can say:

**Quels sont vos loisirs ?**
What are your hobbies?

To talk about your likes and dislikes, you can use the following expressions:

**J'aime** *la cuisine.*
I like cooking.

**J'adore** *les animaux.*
I love animals.

**Je n'aime pas** *le sport.*

I don't like sports.

*Je déteste la lecture.*
I hate reading.

As you might have noticed, these expressions are followed by a noun, preceded by a definite article. This is an important rule to remember: when talking about something in general, for example, sports (*le sport*) or animals (*les animaux*), we always use definite articles.

The expressions above can also be followed by a verb. For example:

*J'aime **cuisiner**.*
I like cooking.

*J'adore **lire**.*
I love reading.

*Je n'aime pas **chanter**.*
I don't like singing.

*Je déteste **danser**.*
I hate dancing.

Note that the second verbs are in the infinitive, meaning they are not conjugated. For example in the sentence *Je n'aime pas chanter*, the verb *chanter* is in the infinitive form. When combining two verbs in French, it is only the first verb that is conjugated.

## GRAMMAR TIP
### Negation

To negate a verb, we simply add the words *ne* or *n'* and *pas*. Use *n'* if the verb starts with a vowel or a silent h. These two elements "sandwich" the main verb. For example:

- *Je chante.* I sing.
- *Je ne chante pas.* I don't sing.

We put *ne* before the verb and *pas* after it. Remember to contract the *ne* before a vowel:

- **J'aime le sport.** I like sports.
- **Je n'aime pas le sport.** I don't like sports.

**Hobbies vocabulary**

|  | Translation |
|---|---|
| *la cuisine* | cooking |
| *la danse* | dancing |
| *la lecture* | reading |
| *la mode* | fashion |
| *la musique* | music |
| *la peinture* | painting |
| *le chant* | singing |
| *le jardinage* | gardening |
| *le sport* | sports |
| *le voyage* | traveling |
| *les jeux vidéo* | video games |

Which of the following activities above do you like doing? Try saying them aloud using the expressions we learned: *j'aime*, *j'adore*, *je n'aime pas* or *je déteste*.

**Tonic pronouns**

Tonic pronouns are used to emphasize the subject of a sentence. For example, we can say:

> **Moi,** *j'aime la cuisine.* **Lui,** *il déteste la cuisine.*
> Me, I like cooking. Him, he hates cooking.

Here are the corresponding tonic pronouns according to the subject:

| Subject | Tonic pronoun |
|---|---|
| je | *moi* |

| tu | *toi* |
|---|---|
| il | *lui* |
| elle | *elle* |
| nous | *nous* |
| vous | *vous* |
| ils | *eux* |
| elles | *elles* |

Let's look at some more examples:

**Eux***, ils adorent le sport*.
Them, they love sports.

**Elle***, elle n'aime pas la lecture.*
Her, she hates reading.

# Talking about one's hobbies

To talk about one's hobbies, we use the verbs *faire* (to do) and *jouer* (to play). These two verbs are not interchangeable. Each one is used with a specific area of activity.

### Sports

The verb *jouer* is generally used to talk about doing sports or playing a musical instrument. When talking about sports, it is followed by the preposition *à*. This preposition, as always, changes according to the gender and number of the noun:

**Je joue au foot.**
I play football.

**Nous jouons au tennis.**
We play tennis.

**Elle aime jouer au volley.**
I like playing volleyball.

*Tu joues aux échecs ?*
Do you play chess?

The preposition *à* changes accordingly:

| For nouns that… | Preposition *à* |
|---|---|
| are feminine | *à la* |
| start with a vowel | *à l'* |
| are masculine | *au* |
| are plural | *aux* |

In Chapter 3, we learned that the preposition *à* changes to *en*, *au* and *aux* before countries. This is only the case with <u>countries</u>. With general nouns, we follow the forms summarized in the table above.

We also use the verb *faire* with sports, usually when it is a sport done alone or when it does not involve the use of tools like ball, bat, etc.

*Nous faisons de la boxe.*
We box.


*Je fais de la natation.*
I swim.


*Louise fait du jogging tous les jours.*
Louise jogs every day.


### Music

When talking about music, we also use the verb *jouer*, but with the preposition *de*:

*Il joue du piano.*
He plays the piano.


*Martin joue de la guitare.*
Martin plays the guitar.

As we learned in the previous chapter, *de* changes according to the gender and number of the noun:

| For nouns that... | Preposition *de* |
|---|---|
| are feminine | *de la* |
| start with a vowel | *de l'* |
| are masculine | *du* |
| are plural | *des* |

---

**GRAMMAR TIP**
**The verb *faire***

The verb faire translates to "to do" or "to make". It is an irregular verb that is conjugated as follows:

|  | **faire** |
|---|---|
| **Je** | fais |
| **Tu** | fais |
| **Il/Elle** | fait |
| **Nous** | faisons |
| **Vous** | faites |
| **Ils/Elles** | font |

---

## *Sports and music vocabulary*

In the vocabulary list below, we included the verbal phrase that goes with each activity. This way, you will best remember whether to use *faire* or *jouer*.

|  | Translation |
|---|---|
| *faire de l'équitation* | to go horseback riding |
| *faire de la boxe* | to box |
| *faire de la natation* | to swim |

| | |
|---|---|
| *faire de la randonnée* | to go mountain climbing |
| *faire du ski* | to ski |
| *faire du vélo* | to bike |
| *jouer au basket* | to play basketball |
| *jouer au foot* | to play football |
| *jouer au tennis* | to play tennis |
| *jouer au volley* | to play volleyball |
| *jouer aux cartes* | to play cards |
| *jouer de la batterie* | to play drums |
| *jouer de la guitare* | to play the guitar |
| *jouer du piano* | to play the piano |
| *jouer du violon* | to play the violin |

## CULTURE TIP
### *Fans of pétanque*

*La pétanque* is a popular French sport played outdoors. There are usually two teams that compete. Each takes turns to throw *une boule*, a metallic ball about the size of an apple, towards a smaller ball called *le cochonnet*. The one who gets it closest to the *cochonnet* gains points.

# Key Takeaways

- To ask or indicate one's hobbies, we use the following expressions:

| Ask one's hobbies | |
|---|---|
| *Quels sont vos loisirs ?* | |
| **Indicate one's hobbies** | |
| *J'aime…*<br>*J'adore…*<br>*Je n'aime*<br>*pas…*<br>*Je déteste…* | + definite article and noun<br>OR<br>+ verb |

- To negate a verb, we simply place it in between *ne* or *n'* and *pas*.
- Tonic pronouns are used to emphasize the subject of a sentence: *moi, toi, lui, elle, nous, vous, eux* and *elles*.
- The verb *jouer* is generally used to talk about sports and music. Before sports-related nouns, we use the preposition *à* (*à l', au, à la, aux*). Before music-related nouns, we use *de* (*de la, de l', du, des*).
- The verb *faire* is used to talk about sports done alone. It is followed by the preposition *de*.
- We conjugate the verb *faire* as follows: *je fais, tu fais, il/elle fait, nous faisons, vous faites, ils/elles font*.

In the next chapter, we move to the realm of food. You will learn how to buy at the market, ask for prices and indicate quantities. We will also study how to say numbers above 100 in French.

# Exercises

1-5. *Faire de, jouer de* or *jouer à*? Complete the sentences with the appropriate verbal phrase. Don't forget to conjugate the verbs and change the prepositions according to the gender and number of the noun.

    1. Sarah_____ski.
    2. Je_____guitare.
    3. Elle aime_____basket.
    4. Tu_____cartes ?
    5. Louise et Nathan_____natation.

6-8. Read the text below and indicate whether the statements are true or false.

*Pierre aime la musique et le sport. Il joue du piano et de la guitare. Le week-end, il joue au foot dans le parc avec ses amis. Parfois, il fait aussi de la natation. Sa femme, Camille, adore aussi la musique. Elle, elle joue du violon.*

6. Both Pierre and his wife can play musical instruments.
7. Camille plays football during weekends.
8. Pierre knows how to swim.

9. Negate the following sentence: *J'aime la peinture.*

10. Negate the following sentence: *Adrien aime la danse.*

# Answer Key

1. fait du
2. joue de la
3. jouer au
4. joues aux
5. font de la
6. True.
7. False. It is Pierre who does.
8. True.
9. Je n'aime pas la peinture.
10. Adrien n'aime pas la danse.

# Chapter 9: Beyond baguettes

*Faute de pain, on mange de la galette.*

For lack of bread, we eat pancakes.

- Quebec proverb

France, a paradise for food-lovers! When one thinks of France, food – bread and cheese in particular – comes to mind. If traveling to France, it would be a foodie's mistake not to try the famous *baguettes* and *croissants* fresh from the oven of a traditional bakery. Those who love fruits would want to visit the *marché* (market) for some fresh produce.

In this lesson, you will learn how to communicate in food-related, buy-and-sell situations. You will learn how to ask for prices and indicate quantities. Finally, we will also study how to read numbers above 100.

## At the bakery

It's 8 a.m. and Pierre goes to a bakery to buy some breakfast:

**Pierre**: *Bonjour Madame.* **Je voudrais** *une baguette, quatre pains au chocolat et une tarte aux fraises.*
**Vendor**: *Bien sûr… **et avec ceci ?***
**Pierre**: **Je vais aussi prendre** *une baguette.*
**Vendor**: *D'accord. **Ce sera tout ?***
**Pierre**: *Oui. **C'est combien s'il vous plaît ?***
**Vendor**: **Ça vous fait** *9 euros.*

We already learned how to use the expression *je voudrais* (I would like) to ask for something in French. Like Pierre, you can also say *je vais aussi prendre* (I will also take) to ask for something else.

It is useful to remember the phrases a vendor might say, so you can reply!

**Et avec ceci ?**
What else would you like? (lit. And with that?)

**Ce sera tout ?**
Would that be all?

**Baked goods vocabulary**

|  | Translation |
|---|---|
| *un croissant* | a croissant |
| *un gâteau* | a cake |
| *un gâteau au chocolat* | a chocolate cake |
| *une baguette* | a baguette |
| *une tarte* | a pie |
| *une tarte aux fraises* | a strawberry pie |
| *une tarte au citron* | a lemon pie |
| *un pain au chocolat* | a chocolate bread |
| *un chausson aux pommes* | an apple turnover |
| *un pain complet* | a whole-wheat bread |
| *un pain de mie* | a sandwich loaf |

Pro tip: flavors in French are generally preceded by the preposition *à*. For example, a lemon pie would be *une tarte **au** citron*, while strawberry ice cream would be *une glace **à la** fraise*.

**Asking or indicating price**

Remember that we previously learned *Combien ça coûte ?* to ask for the price of something. You can also say *C'est combien ?* Or at the counter, you can ask for the total price by saying *Ça fait combien ?* Vendors would often indicate the price using the same expression: *Ça fait … euros.*

# At the fruit stand

Hélène goes to the market to buy some fruits:

**Hélène**: *Bonjour Monsieur, je voudrais 500 grammes de fraises, deux melons et un kilo de pommes.*
**Vendor**: *Voilà Madame. Ce sera tout ?*
**Hélène**: *Oui, merci. Ça fait combien ?*
**Vendor**: *Ça vous fait 17 euros.* ***Vous payez par carte ou en espèces ?***
**Hélène**: ***Je vais payer par carte.***

### Indicating mode of payment

A vendor might ask you how you wish to pay:

***Vous payez par carte ou en espèces ?***
Do you pay by card or with cash?

To which, you can reply:

***Je vais payer par carte.***
I will pay by card.

***Je vais payer en espèces.***
I will pay with cash.

### Indicating quantity

To indicate quantity, we can use the following measure words: *un kilo* (a kilo), *un litre* (a liter), *une douzaine* (a dozen). The term *un demi-kilo* is rarely used to mean "half a kilo", instead we say *500 grammes* (500 grams).

All of these measure words are followed by the preposition *de*. This time, *de* does not change according to the gender and number. It does however contract before a vowel. So for example, *un kilo **de** fraises*, *un kilo **d'**abricots*.

Here are other useful measure words:

| | Translation |
| --- | --- |

| | |
|---|---|
| *un peu de* | a little bit of<br>ex. **un peu de** *persil* (a little bit of parsley) |
| *beaucoup de* | a lot of, many<br>ex. **beaucoup de** *fruits* (a lot of fruits) |
| *une tranche de* | a slice of<br>ex. **une tranche de** *jambon* (a slice of ham) |
| *un morceau de* | a piece of, a slice of<br>ex. **un morceau de** *fromage* (a slice of cheese) |
| *une bouteille de* | a bottle of<br>ex. **une bouteille d'**huile (a bottle of oil) |

## CULTURE TIP
### *The many meanings of baguette*

Did you know that the word *baguette* in French does not only refer to the famous bread? We also call the following *une baguette*:

- A magician's wand
- A musical conductor's baton
- A musical drumstick
- Chopsticks

Like the bread, all of these objects have the same elongated shape! Note that chopsticks are always in plural form, *des baguettes*.

*Fruits and vegetables vocabulary*

| Fruits | Translation |
| --- | --- |
| *des cerises* | cherries |
| *du raisin* | grapes |
| *un abricot* | an apricot |
| *un ananas* | a pineapple |
| *un citron* | a lemon |
| *une banane* | a banana |
| *une fraise* | a strawberry |
| *une orange* | an orange |
| *une pêche* | a peach |
| *une poire* | a pear |
| *une pomme* | an apple |
| Vegetables | Translation |
| *de l'ail* | garlic |
| *des haricots verts* | green beans |
| *un brocoli* | a broccoli |
| *un chou* | a cabbage |
| *un oignon* | an onion |
| *une aubergine* | an eggplant |
| *une carotte* | a carrot |
| *une pomme de terre* | a potato |
| *une salade* | a lettuce |
| *une tomate* | a tomato |

# Numbers 100 above

To count from 100 up, we use the following words:

*cent* 100, hundred
*mille* 1000, thousand
*million* 1 000 000, million
*milliard* 1 000 000 000, billion

Surely no baguette would cost a billion. Still, it is useful to memorize them. To form numbers 100 and above, we follow the same structure in English. Assemble the numbers from biggest to smallest. For example: hundred + tens + units.

100 **cent**
200 **deux-cents**
235 **deux-cent-trente-cinq**
500 **cinq-cents**
555 **cinq-cent-cinquante-cinq**

Notice that the –s in *cents* disappears when followed by other numerals. Let's look at higher numbers:

**1** 000 **mille**
**2** 379 **deux-mille-trois-cent-soixante-dix-neuf**

Or even higher:

2 000 000 **deux-millions**
2 900 110 **deux-millions-neuf-cent-mille-cent-dix**

When indicating a price, the French distinguish cents by placing it after the euros. For example: 10,50€ is read as *dix euros cinquante centimes* or simply, *dix euros cinquante.* In written French, the cent unit is separated with a comma not a period.

## Key Takeaways

- Here are the expressions you must know when buying at the bakery or at the market:

| |
|---|
| *Je voudrais…* <br> *Je vais aussi prendre…* |
| **Ask for price** |
| *C'est combien ?* <br> *Ça fait combien ?* <br> *Combien ça coûte ?* |

| Indicate price |
| --- |
| *Ça fait … euros.* |
| **Ask or indicate mode of payment** |
| *Vous payez par carte ou en espèces ?* |
| *Je vais payer par carte.* |
| *Je vais payer en espèces.* |

- To indicate quantity, we use measure words like *un kilo*, *un litre*, *une douzaine*, *500 grammes*, *un peu de*, *beaucoup de*, *une tranche de*, *un morceau de* and *une bouteille de*. The preposition *de* contracts to *d'* before a vowel but does not change otherwise.
- To count from 100 up, we use the following words: *cent*, *mille*, *million*, *milliard*.
- We form numbers starting with the biggest unit to the smallest.
- To distinguish cents in prices, we say *euros* before the cents.

In the next chapter, we head to the skies. You will learn how to describe the weather and talk about seasons. We will also study some French weather idioms to help you sound like a real native!

# Exercises

1-5. Complete the dialogue with the appropriate missing words:

*aussi – payer – ceci - voudrais – combien*

- Bonjour Monsieur. Je 1.____une baguette s'il vous plaît.
- Et avec 2._____ ?
- Je vais 3._____prendre deux croissants.
- Ce sera tout ?
- Oui, ça fait 4._____ ?
- Cinq euros trente.
- Je vais 5._____en espèces.

6-10. Write the following numbers in words:

6. 800
7. 420
8. 1930
9. 30,75€

10. 40 800

# Answer Key

1. voudrais
2. ceci
3. aussi
4. combien
5. payer
6. huit-cents
7. quatre-cent-vingt
8. mille-neuf-cent-trente
9. trente euros soixante-quinze (centimes)
10. quarante-mille-huit-cents

# Chapter 10: No rain check allowed

*Les raisons d'aimer et de vivre, varient comme font les saisons.*

The reasons for loving and living, vary like the seasons.

- Louis Aragon

One of the most common topics when making small talk is the weather. In fact, in French, there is an expression that directly links small talk to weather: *parler de la pluie et du beau temps*, which means "to make small talk" (the literal translation is "to talk about the rain and the good weather").

In this lesson, you will learn how to ask about and describe the weather. We will also learn the words for seasons in French.

## Weather

### Asking about the weather

To refer to the weather, we can use the words *le temps* or *la météo*. *Le temps* refers to the climate while *la météo* refers to the weather or weather forecast. Note that *le temps* is also the general word for "time".

To ask what the weather's like, we say:

> ***Quel temps fait-il ?*** (for.)
> ***Il fait quel temps ?*** (inf.)
> What's the weather like?

To ask about the temperature, we say:

> ***Quelle température fait-il ?*** (for.)
> ***Il fait quelle température ?*** (inf.)
> What is the temperature?

In France, the Celsius is used. You don't have to specify it though when indicating the temperature.

### Describing the weather

There are three ways to describe the weather. First, using the fixed expression *il fait*:

- *Il fait beau*. The weather is nice.
- *Il fait mauvais*. The weather is bad.
- *Il ne fait pas beau*. The weather is not nice.
- *Il fait chaud*. It's hot.
- *Il fait froid*. It's cold.
- *Il fait 30 degrés*. It's 30 degrees (Celsius).

Don't be tempted to use the verb *être* to describe the weather. While in English, one might say "It is hot", in French, it is incorrect to say *Il est chaud* when referring to the climate. We have to use the expression *il fait*, as in *il fait chaud*.

The second way to describe the weather involves using specific verbs:

- *Il pleut*. It's raining.
- *Il neige*. It's snowing.

Finally, you can use the expression *il y a* with the preposition *de*:

- *Il y a du brouillard*. It's foggy. (lit. There is fog.)
- *Il y a du vent*. It's windy. (lit. There is wind.)
- *Il y a de l'orage*. There's a storm.
- *Il y a des nuages*. It's cloudy. (lit. There are clouds.)
- *Il y a du soleil*. It's sunny. (lit. There is sun.)

By now, you probably know that the preposition *de* changes in form to correspond to the gender and number of the noun it follows.

### Weather vocabulary

Here are other useful vocabularies related to weather:

|  | Translation |
| --- | --- |
| *la lune* | the moon |
| *la grêle* | the hail |

| | |
|---|---|
| *la neige* | the snow |
| *la pluie* | the rain |
| *le soleil* | the sun |
| *le tonnerre* | the thunder |
| *un arc-en-ciel* | a rainbow |
| *un éclair* | a lightning |
| *une étoile* | a star |
| *un thermomètre* | a thermometer |
| *une tempête* | a storm |

## CULTURE TIP
### Some weather idioms

Learning some weather idioms is a great way to sound like a native. We list below three expressions that are used in colloquial French:

- **Il fait un soleil de plomb !**
  The sun is blazing hot.
- **Il pleut des cordes.**
  It's raining heavily. (lit. It's raining ropes)
- **Il fait un froid de canard.**
  It's freezing. (lit. It's duck-like cold)

# Seasons

Let us now talk about *les saisons* (seasons). Read the text below. Can you tell how the four seasons are called in French?

*Au printemps, de mars à juin, il fait beau. Après le printemps, c'est l'été. En été, de juin à septembre, il fait chaud. En automne, de septembre à décembre, les feuilles tombent. En hiver, de décembre à mars, il fait froid.*

In the spring, from March to June, the weather is nice. After spring, it's summer. In summer, from June to September, it is hot. In fall, from September to December, the leaves fall. In winter, from December to March, it is cold.

Did you guess right? The four seasons are:

- **Le printemps** spring
- **L'été** summer
- **L'automne** fall
- **L'hiver** winter

Take note that we use the preposition *en* with the *été, automne* and *hiver*. For *printemps*, the preposition *au* is used:

- **au printemps** in spring
- **en été** in summer
- **en automne** in fall
- **en hiver** in winter

## Key Takeaways

- There are three ways to describe the weather: (1) with *il fait*, (2) with specific verbs and (3) with *il y a*:

| Ask about the weather |
|---|
| *Quel temps fait-il ?* (for.)<br>*Il fait quel temps ?* (inf.) |
| *Quelle température fait-il ?* (for.)<br>*Il fait quelle température ?* (inf.) |

| Describe the weather | |
|---|---|
| **Il fait** | *beau.*<br>*mauvais.*<br>*chaud.*<br>*froid.*<br>*… degrés.* |
| **Il pleut.**<br>**Il neige.** | |

| Il y a | du brouillard. |
|--------|----------------|
|        | du vent. |
|        | de l'orage. |
|        | des nuages. |
|        | du soleil. |

- The four seasons are: *le printemps*, *l'été*, *l'automne* and *l'hiver*. We use the preposition *au* with *printemps*, and *en* with the other three.

In the next chapter, we will talk about time. You will finally be able to use those numbers you memorized from the previous chapters! We will also study the days of the week in French.

# Exercises

1-5. Translate the following sentences:

1. It is sunny.
2. It is hot.
3. The weather is nice.
4. There's a storm.
5. What's the weather like?

6-8. Specify the season being described.

6. The season when people go to the beach.
7. The season when people wear heavy coats.
8. The season when leaves fall.

9. Complete the dialogue with the missing word:

- *Il fait quelle_____ ?*
- *Il fait 23 degrés.*

10. Complete the idiomatic expression: *Il fait un_____de canard!*

# Answer Key

1. Il y a du soleil.
2. Il fait chaud.
3. Il fait beau.
4. Il y a de l'orage.
5. Quel temps fait-il ? OR Il fait quel temps ?
6. En été.
7. En hiver.
8. En automne.
9. température
10. froid

# Chapter 11: The hands of time

*Le temps adoucit tout.*

Time softens everything.

- Voltaire

Time structures our everyday lives. We plan our days by the hour, sometimes even by the minute. We wake up at a certain time, go to work or school at this time, come home at this time; meet up with friends at this time, and so on. Being able to tell the time is thus an important skill to have when learning not just French, but any language.

In this chapter, you will learn how to tell time. We will also study how to indicate dates. Telling time in French is not particularly difficult. Quite often, what intimidates learners is the mastery of numbers required to naturally and speedily read time. Feel free to review the numbers in Chapters 2, 5 and 9 or consult the annex for the complete list.

## Time

We learned in the previous chapter that *le temps* can mean both weather (as in the phrase *il fait quel temps ?*) or time, in the general sense. For instance, to say "I spend my time watching films", you can say *Je passe mon temps à regarder des films*. Or, if someone invites you out but you're busy, you might say *Désolé(e), je n'ai pas le temps* (Sorry, I don't have time.) Le temps is also used in fixed expressions:

- **de temps en temps**  from time to time
- **la plupart du temps**  most of the time
- **pendant ce temps**  during this time.

Now, when we are referring to time as in <u>clock</u> time, we use the term *l'heure* (f.). For example, to ask and tell the time, you use *l'heure* and not *le temps.*

*L'heure* (f.) literally translates to "hour". Minutes in French is *minutes* (f.), while seconds is *secondes* (f.). The C in *secondes* is pronounced like a hard g, like the g in the English word *guitar*.

### Asking the time

To ask what time it is, you can say:

**Quelle heure est-il ?** (for.)
**Il est quelle heure ?** (inf.)
What time is it?

This is a fixed expression. The pronoun *il* never changes. You can also say:

**Vous avez l'heure ?** (for.)
**Tu as l'heure ?** (inf.)
Do you have the time?

### Telling the time

To tell the time, you use the expression *Il est*:

**Il est 12h00.**
It is 12 o'clock.

**Il est 9h30.**
It is 9:30 a.m.

There are a few things to keep in mind:

- French time uses the 24-hour clock military time. So for example, 1 p.m. would be *treize heures* or 13h.
- Note that when written down, French hours are not separated from the minutes with a colon. Instead, the letter h for *heure* is used. For example, 10:30 would be written as *10h30*.
- There are words for a.m. (*du matin*) and p.m. (*de l'après-midi* for until 6 p.m. and *du soir* for later) but they are rarely used. Since we

refer to a 24-hour clock, it is clear that when we say *14h* for example, we mean 2 in the afternoon.

To tell the time, we say *il est* + numbers 1 to 24 + *heures* + number of minutes. While in English, you can omit the "o'clock" and say for instance, "It's 8". In French, you cannot omit the word *heure*. Let's look at some examples:

| | |
|---|---|
| *Il est neuf heures.* | It is 9 a.m. |
| *Il est six heures dix.* | It is 6:10 a.m. |
| *Il est quatorze heures.* | It is 2 p.m. |
| *Il est quinze heures vingt-cinq.* | It is 3:25 p.m. |
| *Il est vingt-deux heures.* | It is 10 p.m. |

We say *midi* for noon and *minuit* for midnight:

| | |
|---|---|
| *Il est midi.* | It is noon. |
| *Il est minuit.* | It is midnight. |

Now, to say "half past", we use the term *demi* or *demie*. "Quarter past" would be *et quart* and "quarter to" would be *moins le quart*. Look at the examples below:

| | |
|---|---|
| *Il est six heures et demie.* | It is 6:30 a.m. |
| *Il est dix heures et demie.* | It is 10:30 a.m. |
| *Il est midi et demi.* | It is 12:30 p.m. |
| *Il est minuit et demi.* | It is 00:30 a.m. |
| *Il est huit heures et quart.* | It is 8:15 a.m. |
| *Il est sept heures moins le quart.* | It is 6:45 a.m. |

Except for *midi* and *minuit*, we always write *demie* with an –e. Note that *demi(e)* can only be used from 1 to 12. Past twelve, we use the word thirty or *trente*:

| | |
|---|---|
| *Il est quatorze heures trente.* | It is 2:30 p.m. |
| *Il est vingt-trois heures trente.* | It is 11:30 p.m. |

For 31 to 59 minutes past the hour, we can use the word *moins* (less) the number of minutes. For example:

| | |
|---|---|
| ***Il est dix heures moins vingt.*** | It is 9:40 a.m. (lit. It is 10 hrs. minus 20.) |
| ***Il est onze heures moins dix.*** | It is 10:50 a.m. (lit. It is 11 hrs. minus 10.) |

When referring to time in general sentences, we use the preposition *à*. For example:

- ***Je finis le travail à 18h.*** I finish work at 6 p.m.
- ***Les enfants rentrent à 15h.*** The kids come home at 3 p.m.

---

**GRAMMAR TIP**
*-IR verbs*

To conjugate regular –IR verbs in the present tense, we simply remove the –ir of the infinitive form and replace them with a set of fixed endings. And so, for example, we remove the –ir in the verb fin*ir* (to finish) and then we add the appropriate endings:

| finir → fin | | |
|---|---|---|
| **Je** | +is | fin**is** |
| **Tu** | +is | fin**is** |
| **Il/Elle/On** | +it | fin**it** |
| **Nous** | +issons | fin**issons** |
| **Vous** | +issez | fin**issez** |
| **Ils/Elles** | +issent | fin**issent** |

---

# Date

### Asking and indicating the day

The word for a day in French is *un jour*. You can ask the day of the week using the following expressions:

*Quel jour sommes-nous aujourd'hui ?* (for.)
*Nous sommes quel jour aujourd'hui ?* (for.)
*On est quel jour aujourd'hui ?* (inf.)
What day is it today?

To indicate the day, we say: *Nous sommes* (for.) or *On est* (inf.) + the day.

**Nous sommes lundi.**
It's Monday (lit. We are Monday.)

**On est mardi.**
It's Tuesday (lit. We are Tuesday.)

### Days of the week vocabulary

|  | Translation |
|---|---|
| *lundi* | Monday |
| *mardi* | Tuesday |
| *mercredi* | Wednesday |
| *jeudi* | Thursday |
| *vendredi* | Friday |
| *samedi* | Saturday |
| *dimanche* | Sunday |

### Asking and indicating the date

The word for the date in French is *la date*. You can ask the date using the following expressions:

**Quelle date sommes-nous aujourd'hui ?** (for.)
**On est quelle date aujourd'hui ?** (inf.)
What date is it today?

To indicate the day, we say: *Nous sommes* (for.) or *On est* (inf.) + the day.

**Nous sommes le 6 octobre.**
It's October 6th.

**On est le 3 janvier.**

It's January 3rd.

For the first day of the month, use the ordinal number *premier*:

**On est le premier mars.**
It's March 1st.

Note that the dates in French are written starting with the day and not the month. They are always preceded by the article *le*. To say your birthdate for example:

**Je suis né(e) le 2 août 1989.**
I was born on August 2nd, 1989.

### Months vocabulary

The word for a month in French is *un mois.* A year is *une année.*

|  | Translation |
|---|---|
| *janvier* | January |
| *février* | February |
| *mars* | March |
| *avril* | April |
| *mai* | May |
| *juin* | June |
| *juillet* | July |
| *août* | August |
| *septembre* | September |
| *octobre* | October |
| *novembre* | November |
| *décembre* | December |

In French, the months are not capitalized. When indicating a month (<u>without</u> the day), we use the preposition *en.* For example, "in January" would be *en janvier*, "in March", *en mars*, and so on.

# Key Takeaways

- *Le temps* refers to time in general while *l'heure* refers to clock time.

- To ask or indicate the time and date, we use the following expressions:

| Ask and tell time | |
|---|---|
| *Quelle heure est-il ? (for.)*<br>*Il est quelle heure ? (inf.)*<br>*Vous avez l'heure ? (for.)*<br>*Tu as l'heure ? (inf.)* | *Il est… heures.* |

| Ask and tell dates | | |
|---|---|---|
| *Quel jour sommes-nous aujourd'hui ? (for.)*<br>*Nous sommes quel jour aujourd'hui ? (for.)*<br>*On est quel jour aujourd'hui ? (inf.)* | *Nous sommes*<br>*On est* | + day |
| *Quelle date sommes-nous aujourd'hui ? (for.)*<br>*On est quelle date aujourd'hui ? (inf.)* | *Nous sommes le*<br>*On est le* | + date |

- We can also indicate time using the fixed expressions: *demi(e)*, *et quart*, *moins le quart* and *moins*.
- The days in French are: *lundi*, *mardi*, *mercredi*, *jeudi*, *vendredi*, *samedi* and *dimanche*.
- The months in French are: *janvier*, *février*, *mars*, *avril*, *mai*, *juin*, *juillet*, *août*, *septembre*, *octobre*, *novembre* and *décembre*. We use the preposition *en* with months.
- To conjugate -IR verbs, we replace the ending with the following: *-is*, *-is*, *-it*, *-issons*, *-issez* and *-issent*.

In the next chapter, you will learn how to talk about your daily routine. You will also learn expressions of time and frequency, alongside pronominal verbs.

# Exercises

1-5. Complete the short dialogues with the missing words:

     *1. - On est quel_____aujourd'hui ?*
      *- On est samedi.*
     *2. - Quelle_____est-il ?*

*- Il est midi.*

*3. - Nous sommes_____date aujourd'hui ?*

*- Nous sommes le 20 mai.*

*4. - Tu as l'heure ?*

*- Oui,_____est 13 heures.*

*5. - Nous sommes quel jour aujourd'hui ?*

*- Nous_____mercredi.*

6-10. Write the following times in words:

6. It's 3 p.m.
7. It's 4:45 a.m.
8. It's noon.
9. It's 7:30 a.m.
10. It's 6:30 p.m.

# Answer Key

1. jour
2. heure
3. quelle
4. il
5. sommes
6. Il est quinze heures.
7.  Il est cinq heures moins le quart. OR Il est quatre heures quarante-cinq.
8. Il est midi.
9. Il est sept heures et demie.
10. Il est dix-huit heures trente.

# Chapter 12: An ordinary day

*L'habitude est une seconde nature.*

Habit is second nature.

- Augustin D'Hippone

If time structures our lives, habits are the ones that constitute them. For most people, the order of the day is clear. They wake up, eat breakfast, brush their teeth, take a shower then go to work or school, then come back home. Routines, schedules and habits are what organize our days.

In this lesson, you will learn how to talk about your daily routine. In order to do so, you would need to master pronominal verbs and expressions of frequency.

## Talking about daily habits

In the text below, Pierre describes his daily routine:

*__Je me réveille__ tous les jours à 8h. Ensuite, __je me lève__… __Je me prépare__ pour aller au travail : __je me douche, je me rase__ et __je m'habille__. Je prends mon petit-déjeuner, puis __je me brosse__ les dents. Je vais au travail à 9h. Je rentre vers 18h. Le soir, __je me repose__ devant un film. Je dîne. Puis, à 22h, __je me couche__.*

I wake up every day at 8 a.m. Then I get up… I get ready to go to work: I shower, I shave and I get dressed. I eat my breakfast, then I brush my teeth. I go to work at 9 a.m. I come back at around 6 p.m. In the evening, I rest in front of a movie. I eat dinner. Then, at 10 p.m., I go to bed.

The verbs in bold are what we call "pronominal verbs". You already encountered one in the first chapter, the verb *s'appeler*.

There are a lot of pronominal verbs used when talking about daily routines. To start, what are they?

### Pronominal verbs

In English, there are no pronominal verbs. In French, these are verbs combined with pronouns, hence the appellation *pronominal*. These verbs are always composed of two parts, a pronoun and a verb. They are reflexive, meaning the action or verb is done to the subject of the sentence. Look at these two sentences:

**Je me douche.** I take a shower.
**Je douche...** I shower...

The first one has the pronominal verb *me doucher* which literally means, "to shower myself". So, *je me douche* means, "I take a shower". The second one means: I shower... probably someone else! Without the reflexive pronoun *me*, you will be saying that you're giving someone else a bath!

Remember that not all verbs in French are pronominal. Let's look at other verbs within this category:

| | Translation |
|---|---|
| *s'endormir* | to fall asleep |
| *s'habiller* | to get dressed |
| *se coucher* | to go to bed |
| *se déshabiller* | to undress |
| *se doucher* | to take a shower |
| *se lever* | to get up |
| *se maquiller* | to put makeup on |
| *se préparer* | to get ready |
| *se raser* | to shave oneself |
| *se reposer* | to rest |
| *se réveiller* | to wake up |

How then do we conjugate pronominal verbs? Just like *s'appeler*, the reflexive pronoun changes according to the subject. The verb is then conjugated according to its ending. For example:

|  | *se réveiller* |
| :---: | :---: |
| **Je** | me réveille |
| **Tu** | te réveilles |
| **Il/Elle** | se réveille |
| **Nous** | nous réveillons |
| **Vous** | vous réveillez |
| **Ils/Elles** | se réveillent |

### *Daily activities vocabulary*

Here are other daily activities you should remember:

|  | Translation |
| :--- | :--- |
| *aller à l'école* | to go to school |
| *aller à l'université* | to go to the university |
| *aller à la fac* | to go to the university (slang) |
| *aller au travail* | to go to work |
| *boire du café* | to drink coffee |
| *déjeuner* | to eat lunch |
| *dîner* | to eat dinner |
| *lire le journal* | to read the newspaper |
| *manger* | to eat |
| *prendre le petit-déjeuner* | to eat breakfast |
| *regarder la télé* | to watch TV |
| *rentrer* | to go home |

## GRAMMAR TIP
### The verb *aller*

The verb *aller* means "to go". It is an irregular verb that is conjugated as follows:

|  | **aller** |
| :---: | :---: |

106

| | |
|---|---|
| **Je** | vais |
| **Tu** | vas |
| **Il/Elle** | va |
| **Nous** | allons |
| **Vous** | allez |
| **Ils/Elles** | vont |

Let's look at this verb in context:

- *Je vais au travail à 8h.* I go to work at 8 a.m.
- *Vous allez au cinéma ?* Are you going to the cinema?
- *Nous allons au parc.* We are going to the park.

# Indicating frequency

When talking about habits, it is essential to know expressions of time and adverbs of frequency.

## *Expressions of time*

To indicate the moments of the day, we can say:

- *le matin* in the morning
- *l'après-midi* in the afternoon
- *le soir* in the evening

Other common expressions include:

- *tôt* early
- *tard* late
- *maintenant* right now
- *plus tard* later
- *aujourd'hui* today
- *hier* yesterday
- *demain* tomorrow

## *Adverbs of frequency*

|  | Translation |
|---|---|
| *de temps en temps* | from time to time |
| *d'habitude* | usually |
| *fréquemment* | frequently, often |
| *en général* | generally |
| *généralement* | |
| *parfois* | sometimes |
| *rarement* | rarely, seldom |
| *toujours* | always |
| *tous les jours* | everyday |
| *tous les lundis* | every Monday |
| *tous les mois* | every month |

| | |
|---|---|
| *toutes les semaines* | every week |
| *une fois par semaine* | once a week |
| *deux fois par semaine* | twice a week |

In general, adverbs in French are placed after the verb. For example, we can say:

*Je me maquille **rarement.***
I rarely put makeup on.

*Lucile lit **toujours** le journal.*
Lucile always reads the newspaper.

However, certain adverbs like *d'habitude*, *généralement*, *en général* and *parfois* are placed at the beginning of the sentence.

***D'habitude,** je prends mon petit-déjeuner à 7h.*
Usually, I have breakfast at 7 a.m.

***Parfois,** elle se réveille tard.*
Sometimes, she wakes up late.

---

**CULTURE TIP**
*Such a chore!*

While pretty much no one likes doing chores, our daily life is filled with them. Let's look at some common expressions related to housekeeping:

- ***faire la lessive*** to do laundry
- ***faire la vaisselle*** to do the dishes
- ***faire les courses*** to go grocery shopping
- ***passer l'aspirateur*** to vacuum
- ***ranger*** to clean up, to organize
- ***sortir la poubelle*** to take out the garbage

---

# Key Takeaways

- Pronominal verbs are often used when describing one's daily routine. They are composed of two elements, a pronoun and a verb. To conjugate, the pronouns *me, te, se, nous, vous* and *se* are added to the verb.
- The verb *aller* is conjugated as follows: *je vais, tu vas, il/elle va, nous allons, vous allez, ils/elles vont.*
- The moments of the day are: *le matin, l'après-midi* and *le soir.*
- Other time expressions include: *tôt, tard, maintenant, plus tard, aujourd'hui, hier* and *demain.*
- Adverbs of frequency are placed after the verb, except for *d'habitude, généralement, en général* and *parfois.*

Are you a social butterfly? In the next chapter, we will talk about inviting someone out and accepting or refusing invitations. We will also study modal verbs and the imperative mood.

## Exercises

1-5. Conjugate the indicated pronominal verbs:

1. *Je (**se doucher**)_____tous les jours.*
2. *Anne, tu (**se brosser**)_____les dents maintenant !*
3. *Nous (**se préparer**)_____tôt le matin.*
4. *Véronique (**se maquiller**)_____souvent.*
5. *Ils (**se raser**)_____toutes les semaines.*

6-10. Translate the following sentences.

6. I go to work every day at 7 a.m.
7. Usually, she wakes up early.
8. The children brush their teeth every day.
9. I do the laundry every week.
10. Do you go to bed late?

# Answer Key

1. me douche
2. te brosses
3. nous préparons
4. se maquille
5. se rasent
6. Je vais au travail tous les jours à 7h.
7. D'habitude, elle se réveille tôt.
8. Les enfants se brossent les dents tous les jours.
9. Je fais la lessive toutes les semaines.
10. Tu te couches tard ? OR Vous vous couchez tard ?

# Chapter 13: How about a drink?

*Il n'y a pas d'ami, il n'y a que des moments d'amitié.*

There are no friends, there are only moments of friendship.

- Jules Renard

We learn a language not simply to communicate, but to connect with people. From the previous chapters, you now know how to talk about yourself, your city and your family, discuss hobbies or find common interests with someone. You can now handle first-meeting conversations with ease. But in order to cultivate the new relationships you make, you'd need to spend more time with your new *ami(e)* (friend), perhaps, invite them for a drink or to a party.

In this lesson, you will learn how to invite someone out and how to accept or refuse invitations. We will study how to formulate questions in French using interrogative pronouns. We will also have a look at the three modal verbs: *vouloir* (to want), *pouvoir* (to be able to) and *devoir* (to have to).

## Asking someone out

Let's begin with a dialogue. Mathis calls Lucile and invites her for a drink with friends:

**Mathis** : *Qu'est-ce que tu fais ce week-end ? Tu veux sortir samedi ?*
**Lucile** : *Samedi soir ? Je ne peux pas. Je dois travailler.*
**Mathis** : *Et vendredi ? Tu es dispo ?*
**Lucile** : *Oui, vendredi ça me va ! On va où ?*
**Mathis** : *On peut aller dans un bar avec mes amis, prendre un verre ?*
**Lucile** : *Ça marche ! On se retrouve où ?*
**Mathis** : *On se retrouve à 19h devant le métro Place d'Italie ?*

**Lucile** : *OK, 19h ce vendredi !*

Let's look at the questions posed by Mathis. To ask someone out, we can say:

**Qu'est-ce que tu fais ce week-end ?**
What are you doing this weekend?

Remember that we previously learned the interrogative expression *qu'est-ce que* (what). This pronoun can be used in both formal and informal situations. Note that the *que* contracts to *qu'* before a vowel. For example, *qu'est-ce __qu'__elle fait* (what is she doing).

In <u>very</u> informal situations, you can also say:

**Tu fais quoi ce week-end ?**
What are you doing this weekend?

Alternatively, you can also ask if someone is free using the following expressions:

**Est-ce que tu es disponible ce soir ?**
**Tu es disponible ce soir ?**
**Tu es dispo ce soir ?**
Are you free tonight ?

All the three questions above mean the same. What is the difference? The first with the expression *est-ce que*, is slightly informal. The second is informal and the last is <u>very</u> informal (the slang for *disponible* is *dispo*).

Finally, we can also ask somebody out using the verb vouloir:

**Tu veux sortir ce samedi ?**
Do you want to go out this Saturday?

**Tu veux aller boire un verre ?**
Do you want to go have a drink (with me)?

### The verb vouloir

The verb *vouloir* means to want to. We have actually seen this verb in its conditional mood before, in the expression *je voudrais*. *Vouloir* is an irregular verb that is conjugated in the present tense as follows:

| vouloir | |
|---|---|
| **Je** | veux |
| **Tu** | veux |
| **Il/Elle** | veut |
| **Nous** | voulons |
| **Vous** | voulez |
| **Ils/Elles** | veulent |

Remember that when two verbs are used, only the first verb is conjugated. Let's look at some examples:

- *Je veux sortir avec mes amis.* I want to go out with my friends.
- *Lucas et Sophie veulent regarder un film.* Lucas and Sophie want to watch a film.
- *Tu veux aller en boîte ?* Do you want to go clubbing?

### Social activities vocabulary

| | Translation |
|---|---|
| *aller au restaurant* | go to the restaurant |
| *aller en boîte* | to go clubbing |
| *assister à un match de foot* | to attend a football match |
| *assister à un concert* | to attend a concert |
| *assister à une fête* | to attend a party |
| *boire un verre* | to have a drink |
| *dîner* | to dine |
| *prendre un verre* | to have a drink |
| *sortir* | to go out |
| *un bar* | a bar, a pub |

| | |
|---|---|
| *une boîte (de nuit)* | a club |
| *une fête* | a party |
| *une pendaison de crémaillère* | a housewarming party |
| *une sortie* | an outing |
| *visiter un musée* | to visit a museum |
| *voir un film* | to watch a movie |
| *voir une pièce de théâtre* | to see a play |

## GRAMMAR TIP
### The pronoun *on*

In the dialogue above, we see Lucile say: *On se retrouve où ?* for "Where do we meet?" We learned that the pronoun "we" in French is *nous*, so what is this *on* doing here?

*On* is a subject pronoun that may refer to one of these:

1. The informal variation of "we".
2. "somebody" or "someone".
3. "people in general".

Let's look at some examples:

1. **On va au restaurant.** We are going to the restaurant (inf.).
2. **On vous appelle.** Someone is calling you.
3. **En France, on aime boire du vin.** In France, people like drinking wine.

Take note that *on* is conjugated the same way as *il* and *elle*.

# Accepting or refusing invitations

To accept invitations, we can simply say:

**Oui, je suis disponible.**
Yes, I am available.

**Oui, ça me va.**
Yes, that works for me. (inf.)

You can also use informal expressions of agreement like *OK, d'accord* (Okay) or *ça marche* (that works). Note that *ça marche* is slang, and very informal.

In the dialogue above, Lucile says she can't go out Saturday night. Let's review that part:

**Samedi soir ? Je ne peux pas. Je dois travailler.**
Saturday night? I can't. I have to work.

To refuse an invitation, you can say:

**Je ne peux pas.**
I can't.

**Je ne suis pas disponible.**
**Je ne suis pas dispo.** (inf.)
I'm not available.

You can give an excuse (or make up one!) using the verb *devoir* which means "to have to":

**Je dois rencontrer un ami.**
I have to meet a friend.

**Je dois rester chez moi.**

I have to stay at home.

### The verb pouvoir

The verb *pouvoir* means to be able to. It is conjugated in the present tense as such:

| pouvoir | |
|---|---|
| **Je** | peux |
| **Tu** | peux |
| **Il/Elle** | peut |
| **Nous** | pouvons |
| **Vous** | pouvez |
| **Ils/Elles** | peuvent |

Let's look at some examples:

- *Je peux t'aider si tu veux.* I can help you if you want.
- *Tu peux me réveiller dans une heure ?* Can you wake me up in an hour?
- *On peut se retrouver devant le café.* We can meet up in front of the coffee shop.

Note that the verb *pouvoir* is not used with skills, unlike in English. You can say for example "I can swim" in English, but in French, you need to use the verb "to know", which is *savoir: Je sais nager* (I can swim).

### The verb devoir

The verb *devoir* means to have to. To conjugate in the present tense:

| devoir | |
|---|---|
| **Je** | dois |
| **Tu** | dois |
| **Il/Elle** | doit |
| **Nous** | devons |
| **Vous** | devez |
| **Ils/Elles** | doivent |

Let's look at some examples:

- *Je dois partir.* I have to leave.
- *Anne doit étudier.* Anne has to study.
- *On doit manger.* We have to eat.

# Formulating questions

We have seen two ways to form questions, using *est-ce que* and *qu'est-ce que*. In learning question-formulation in French, it is important to understand the difference between closed and open questions.

Closed questions are questions we can answer with "yes" or "no". All the rest are open questions:

- *Tu es français ?* Are you French? (closed)
- *Vous allez au parc ?* Are you going to the park? (closed)
- *Qu'est-ce que tu fais ?* What are you doing? (open)
- *Nous partons quand ?* When are we leaving? (open)
- *Pourquoi apprenez-vous le français ?* Why are you learning French? (open)

### Closed questions

There are three ways to formulate closed questions. We list them here from the informal to the most formal way:

1. Add a question mark to the end of a declarative sentence and pronounce it with a rising intonation.
2. Start the question with *est-ce que*.
3. Invert the subject and verb and place a hyphen in between.

For example, you want to ask someone, "Are you free tomorrow?". You can thus say it three ways:

1. *Vous êtes disponible ?*
2. *Est-ce que vous êtes disponible ?*
3. *Êtes-vous disponible ?*

Let's look at another example. This time, you want to ask "Does she ski?":

1. *Elle fait du ski ?*
2. *Est-ce qu'elle fait du ski ?*

118

3. ***Fait-elle*** *du ski ?*

*Est-ce que* has no specific translation in English. Think of it as an expression that signals to the listener that you are posing a question and not a declarative sentence. It's quite similar to the word "do", as in "<u>Do</u> you work?" <u>*Est-ce que*</u> *tu travailles?* Note that before a vowel *est-ce que* contracts to *est-ce qu'*.

### Open questions

When you're asking what, when, why, how, etc., you are posing an open question. Just like in English, we use question words in French for open questions. Again, there are three ways we can formulate these questions, from the informal to the most formal way:

1. Add a question word to the declarative sentence.
2. Question word + *est-ce que* + declarative sentence.
3. Question word + subject-verb inversion.

Let's examine how these questions would look like. We take as an example the question "Where are you going?":

1. *Vous allez où ?*
2. *Où est-ce que vous allez ?*
3. *Où allez-vous ?*

The question word here is *où* (where). Let's look at another example, this time with *quand* (when). All of the sentences below translate to "When does she leave?":

1. *Elle part quand ?*
2. *Quand est-ce qu'elle part ?*
3. *Quand part-elle ?*

### Question words

Below is a list of question words. In formal grammar, we call them interrogative adjectives:

| | Translation |
| --- | --- |
| | |

| | |
|---|---|
| combien | how much, how many |
| comment | how |
| d'où | from where |
| où | where |
| pourquoi | why |
| quand | when |

---

**CULTURE TIP**
***My love, my cabbage***

How do you feel about calling your partner a cabbage? A bit odd, right? Well, in France, it's just another common term of endearment. Let's look at some other terms French speakers use to call their special someone:

- ***mon amour*** my love
- ***mon chéri / ma chérie*** my darling
- ***mon chou*** my cabbage
- ***mon ange*** my angel

---

# Key Takeaways

- To ask someone out, accept or refuse invitations, we use the following expressions:

| Ask someone out |
|---|
| *Qu'est-ce que tu fais ce week-end ?* |
| *(Est-ce que) tu es disponible ce soir ?* |
| *Tu veux sortir ce* + day *?* |
| *Tu veux* + activity *?* |

| Accept invitation |
|---|
| *Oui, je suis disponible.* |
| *Oui, ça me va.* |
| *OK.* |
| *D'accord.* |
| *Ça marche !* |

- The verb *vouloir* is conjugated as follows: *je veux, tu veux, il/elle/on veut, nous voulons, vous voulez, ils/elles veulent.*
- The verb *pouvoir*: *je peux, tu peux, il/elle/on peut, nous pouvons, vous pouvez, ils/elles peuvent.*
- The verb *devoir*: *je dois, tu dois, il/elle/on doit, nous devons, vous devez, ils/elles doivent.*
- The pronoun *on* can mean: an informal "we", "someone" or "somebody", or "people" in general.
- To formulate closed questions we can: put a question mark at the end of a declarative sentence, add *est-ce que* at the beginning, or invert the subject and verb.
- To formulate open questions we can: add a question word to a declarative sentence, add question word and *est-ce que*, or invert the subject and verb.
- The question words are: *combien, comment, d'où, où, pourquoi* and *quand.*

In the next chapter, we will talk about eating out. You will learn how to order in a restaurant. We will also study the pronoun *en*.

# Exercises

1-5. Complete the sentence with the correct conjugation of the indicated modal verb.

1. Tu (**vouloir**)_____sortir demain ?
2. On (**devoir**)_____faire la lessive.
3. Nous (**pouvoir**)_____payer en ligne ?
4. Véronique et Jules (**devoir**)_____partir bientôt.
5. Ils (**vouloir**)_____voir une pièce de théâtre.

6-8. Translate this question the three ways we learned: *Vous êtes disponibles ce soir ?*

6. _____

7. _____

8. _____

9. Complete the sentence with the missing word: *Qu'est-ce_____tu fais mardi soir?*

10. Transform the sentence to informal using the pronoun *on*: *Nous aimons le sport !*

# Answer Key

1. veux
2. doit
3. pouvons
4. doivent
5. veulent
6 - 8. Vous êtes disponibles ce soir ? / Est-ce que vous êtes disponibles ce soir / Êtes-vous disponibles ce soir ?
9. que
10. On aime le sport !

# Chapter 14: The art of French dining

*L'appétit vient en mangeant, la soif s'en va en buvant.*

Appetite comes by eating, thirst leaves by drinking.

- Rabelais

If our discussion about buying food in Chapter 9 left you hungry for more (pun fully intended), look no further – for in this lesson, we go back to the world of gastronomy. After learning how to invite someone out in the previous chapter, you've decided to call up a French friend to hang out. Said friend invites you to dine at a restaurant. You panic because you don't know yet how to order in French. Until of course, you open this chapter.

In this lesson, you will learn how to politely order in a restaurant and how to get the check. We will also study the pronoun *en*.

## At the restaurant

### Ordering

If you have a reservation, you can specify this by saying:

**J'ai une réservation au nom de + your surname or full name.**
I have a reservation under the name…

You will be given the menu, called *la carte* in French. The waiter will usually come back after some time to take your order, using any of the expressions below:

- **Vous avez choisi ?** Have you chosen (from the menu)?
- **Qu'est-ce que vous désirez ?** What would you like ?
- **Vous désirez ?** What would you like?

To order in a restaurant, you can use the expressions we previously learned: *je voudrais* and *je vais prendre*. To specify *la cuisson* (lit. cooking) of your steak, you use the following terms: *bleu* (very rare), *saignant* (rare), *à point* (medium-rare) or *bien cuit* (well done).

### Meat vocabulary

|  | Translation |
| --- | --- |
| *de la viande* | meat |
| *du boeuf* | beef |
| *un steak* | a steak |
| *de l'agneau (m.)* | lamb |
| *du porc* | pork |
| *du poulet* | chicken |
| *de la dinde* | turkey |
| *du canard* | duck |
| *du saumon* | salmon |
| *du thon* | tuna |
| *des fruits de mer (m.)* | seafood |
| *des moules (f.)* | mussels |

Pro tip: In French, food in unspecified quantity is preceded by the partitive article *de*: *de l'* (before vowel or h), *du* (m.) *de la* (f.) and *des* (pl.) .

---

**CULTURE TIP**
*French meals take forever*

A meal is called *un repas*. In a French household, you'd hear one call out *À table !* just before meal time. This expression means "it is time to eat" or "the meal is ready". Its literal translation is "to the table". Before eating, one would usually say *Bon appétit* (enjoy your meal).

If invited to eat at a French home, you'd find that the meals are exceptionally long and can last for hours! That is because meals are

---

considered small social gatherings – a time to chat and dine. A dinner might start with *un apéro* (aperitif or pre-dinner drink). Drinks will be served as well as appetizers like chips, *saucissons* (dried sausage), or olives. You'll be tempted to munch a lot, but don't! The real meal is yet to start. Traditionally an *apéro* will be followed by a first course like salad, the main course and the dessert. To finish the meal, the French also often take a cup of coffee.

### Dining vocabulary

|  | Translation |
|---|---|
| *choisir* | to choose |
| *commander* | to order |
| *l'addition (f.)* | the check, the bill |
| *l'eau (f.)* | water |
| *la carte* | the menu |
| *le plat du jour* | the dish of the day |
| *payer* | to pay |
| *réserver* | to reserve |
| *un dessert* | a dessert |
| *un menu* | a special, a set meal |
| *un plat* | a dish |
| *un plat principal* | a main dish, a main course |
| *une boisson* | a drink |
| *une carafe* | a carafe, a jug |
| *une entrée* | an appetizer |
| *une formule* | a set meal |

### Paying

After finishing a meal, you'd want to pay of course! To ask for the bill, you can say:

**Je voudrais l'addition s'il vous plaît.**
I would like the check please.

Or simply:

**L'addition s'il vous plaît.**
The check please.

Do you remember how to ask or indicate the preferred mode of payment? You might be asked *Vous payez par carte ou en espèces ?* To which you can reply, *Je vais payer par carte* or *Je vais payer en espèces.*

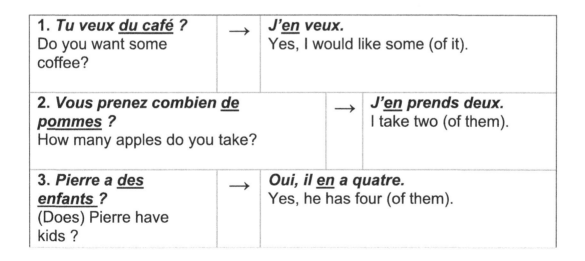

| 1. *Tu veux <u>du café</u> ?* Do you want some coffee? | → | *J'<u>en</u> veux.* Yes, I would like some (of it). |
|---|---|---|
| 2. *Vous prenez combien <u>de pommes</u> ?* How many apples do you take? | → | *J'<u>en</u> prends deux.* I take two (of them). |
| 3. *Pierre a <u>des enfants</u> ?* (Does) Pierre have kids ? | → | *Oui, il <u>en</u> a quatre.* Yes, he has four (of them). |

In example 1, one asks *tu veux du café*, and instead of repeating the noun by replying *je veux du café,* we replace *du café* with the pronoun *en*. You can think of *en* as "some of something". Remember that *en* is always placed before the verb.

*En* is also used to indicate the quantity. We place the number after the verb, as in examples 2 and 3. Here's another example:

**4. *Jean prend trois <u>pommes</u>.*** $\longrightarrow$ ***Jean <u>en</u> prend trois.***

Notice how *pommes* (apples) is replaced by the pronoun *en*. The quantity *trois* (three) is placed after the verb.

## Key Takeaways

- To communicate in a restaurant, we use the following expressions:

| Entering and ordering |
| --- |
| *J'ai une réservation au nom de* + your surname or full name. |
| *Vous avez choisi ?* <br> *Qu'est-ce que vous désirez ?* <br> *Vous désirez ?* |
| *Je voudrais…* <br> *Je vais prendre…* |
| **Paying** |
| *Je voudrais l'addition s'il vous plaît.* <br> *L'addition s'il vous plaît.* |

- The pronoun *en* is used to replace a noun preceded by the preposition *de*. It is placed before the verb.
- We can also specify the quantity with *en*, by placing the number after the verb.

In the next chapter, we will talk about giving and asking directions. We will also study the imperative mood to give commands.

# Exercises

1-2. Complete the dialogue with the appropriate missing words:

     - Bonjour Madame, vous avez 1._____?

     - Oui, je vais 2._____deux plats du jour.

3. Complete the dialogue with the appropriate missing words:

     - 3. Quelle_____pour votre steak ?

     - Saignant, s'il vous plaît.

4-8. Replace the underlined noun with *en*, following the example.

     ex. *Je veux <u>du café</u>.* → <u>  J'en veux </u>.

     4. Claire prend <u>des bananes</u>._____.

     5. Nous avons <u>trois enfants</u>._____.

     6. Tu prends <u>des tomates</u> ?_____.

     7.  Sophie et Éric ont dix <u>stylos</u>._____.

     8. On a deux kilos <u>d'abricots</u>._____.

9. How would you ask for the bill in French?

10. How would you say you have a reservation at a restaurant?

# Answer Key

1. choisi
2. prendre
3. cuisson
4. Claire en prend.
5. Nous en avons trois.
6. Tu en prends ?
7. Sophie et Éric en ont dix.
8. On en a deux kilos.
9. Je voudrais l'addition s'il vous plaît. OR L'addition s'il vous plaît.
10.  Sample answer: J'ai une réservation au nom de (Monique) Dupont.

# Chapter 15: At the crossroads

*Qui s'effraie d'un nuage ne fait pas long voyage.*

He who is frightened by a cloud does not travel long.

- French proverb

If you are big on traveling, odds are you've already found yourself lost in the middle of nowhere once or twice. You got too caught up on the beauty of everything that you've walked too far from where your tour group is supposed to meet up. For the first 5 minutes you panic. And then for about 10 minutes you convince yourself it's all part of the adventure. But after one hour of fatigue and thirst, you start to wish you can just magically acquire the linguistic capacity to, quite simply, ask for directions.

In this lesson, you will learn how to ask directions and understand them. We'll have a look at the imperative mood as well as the conjugation of -RE verbs.

## Asking for directions

You would want to start with a polite *Excusez-moi* or *Pardon*. For example:

**Excusez-moi, Madame. Je cherche la station de métro Olympiades ?**
Excuse me, madam. I'm looking for the subway station Olympiades?

**Pardon, Madame. Je pense que je suis perdu(e). Pourriez-vous m'aider?**
Pardon me, madam. I think I'm lost. Could you please help me?

Alternatively, you can pose direct questions:

**Pardon, Monsieur. Où est la station de métro Olympiades ?**
Pardon me, sir. Where is the subway station Olympiades?

*Excusez-moi, Madame. Pourriez-vous m'indiquer la rue Emile Zola ?*
Excuse me, madam. Could you point me to the Emile Zola street?

# Giving directions

Just as important as knowing how to ask for directions is understanding them when they are given!

Imagine that someone gives you directions to the Olympiades subway station:

*Vous n'êtes pas dans la bonne direction. Prenez la deuxième rue à droite, traversez le pont, puis continuez tout droit. Descendez vers la cathédrale Saint-Pierre. Tournez à gauche. Montez l'avenue Montaigne. Au carrefour, vous allez voir la station de métro, juste à côté du restaurant Chez Jean.*

You are not in the right direction. Take the second street to the right, cross the bridge, then go straight. Go down to the Saint-Pierre Cathedral. Turn left. Go up the Montaigne Avenue. At the intersection, you are going to see the subway station, just beside the Chez Jean restaurant.

Let us break down some of these expressions. To say go straight, we can say:

- *Allez tout droit.*
- *Continuez tout droit.*

To indicate a turn, we can say:

- *Tournez à gauche.*
- *Tournez à droite.*
- *Prenez à gauche.*
- *Prenez à droite.*

*À gauche* means to the left and *à droite*, to the right.

One may also indicate the street to take by saying:

- *Prenez la rue Emile Zola.*
- *Prenez la première rue à gauche.*

- *Prenez la deuxième rue à droite.*

Like in English, the ordinal numbers are used here, as in "first street to the left", or "second street to the right".

If the road is uphill or downhill, we can also use the verbs *monter* (to go up) and *descendre* (to go down).

- *Montez la rue Emile Zola.*
- *Descendez l'avenue Montaigne.*

If it's not accessible by walking, you might also be advised to take public transport. Take note of the following expressions:

- *aller à pied*   go by foot
- *aller en bus / en train / en métro*  go by bus / by train / by subway
- *prendre le train / le bus / le métro* take the train / bus / subway

The verbs used to give directions are usually in the imperative mood. This is why the subject is omitted. We'll learn this in a while. Take note however that sometimes, the present tense form can be used to give directions. So instead of saying *Continuez tout droit*, one can also say *Vous continuez tout droit* or *Tu continues tout droit*.

| descendre → *descend* | | |
|---|---|---|
| **Je** | +s | descend**s** |
| **Tu** | +s | descend**s** |
| **Il/Elle/On** | (none) | descend |
| **Nous** | +ons | descend**ons** |
| **Vous** | +ez | descend**ez** |

| Ils/Elles | +ent | descend**ent** |

Note that irregular verbs do not follow this rule. An example is the verb *prendre* (to take):

| prendre | |
|---|---|
| **Je** | prends |
| **Tu** | prends |
| **Il/Elle/On** | prend |
| **Nous** | prenons |
| **Vous** | prenez |
| **Ils/Elles** | prennent |

For a list of basic verb conjugations, don't forget to consult the annex of this book.

### *Directions vocabulary*

Here are other useful expressions to remember:

| Verbs | Translation |
|---|---|
| *se trouver* | to be located at |
| *aller à* | to go to |
| *aller jusqu'à* | to go until |
| *tourner* | to turn (left or right) |
| *prendre* | to take, to turn (left or right) |
| *traverser* | to cross |
| *revenir* | to come back |
| *retourner* | to return |
| *monter* | to go up |
| *descendre* | to go down |

| Position | Translation |
|---|---|
| *sur votre gauche* | to your left |
| *sur votre droite* | to your right |

| | |
|---|---|
| *au bout de (la rue)* | at the end of (the street) |
| *avant* | before |
| *après* | after |
| *au carrefour* | at the intersection |
| *dans la rue* | in the street |
| *sur le boulevard* | on the boulevard |
| *sur l'avenue* | on the avenue |
| *au feu* | at the stoplight |

### Giving orders

To give orders, we conjugate verbs in what we call the imperative mood. This mood is not only used when giving directions. The imperative in French is similar to English, in that it is used to give a command, an advice, or even a warning. Let's look at some examples:

- (command) ***Fais tes devoirs!*** Do your homework!
- (advice) ***Sois content de ce que tu as.*** Be happy with what you have.
- (warning) ***Ne fumez pas ici.*** Don't smoke here.

The imperative mood has three forms which correspond to the subject pronouns *tu*, *vous* and *nous*. The conjugation is simple: we just take the present tense conjugations of these pronouns and remove the subject. The only exception is for -ER verbs. When conjugated in the *tu* form, we remove the -s.

Say, you want to order someone to close the door. In formal settings, you will use the *vous*-form of the imperative. So, we just take the usual present conjugation of that verb and omit the subject:

***Fermez la porte.***
Close the door.

A quick warning though, you might want to add a *s'il vous plait* at the end of this sentence unless you want to sound mean!

Here's another example, this time with the verb *faire*. We learned that to conjugate *faire* in the second person present tense, we say *fais*. So, if we want to say "do the dishes" informally, we would again follow this conjugation:

**Fais la vaisselle.**
Do the dishes.

Now, for -ER verbs, we remove the -s in the imperative form. Do you remember how to conjugate *parler* (to speak) with *tu*?

A+ for you if you answered *parles*! In the imperative mood, we need to remove the -s:

**Parle plus fort !**
Speak louder!

Finally, we have the *nous* form. This is the equivalent of the English "let's". Again, we just take the present tense conjugation of the verb. So if you want to say "let's go to the park":

**Allons au parc !**
Let's go to the park!

# Key Takeaways

- To ask for directions, we say *Excusez-moi / Pardon + Madame / Monsieur* and the following expressions:

| Ask for directions |
| --- |
| *Je cherche la station de métro Olympiades ?* <br> *Je pense que je suis perdu(e). Pourriez-vous m'aider ?* <br> *Où est la station de métro Olympiades ?* <br> *Pourriez-vous m'indiquer la rue Emile Zola ?* |

- To give directions, we use the following expressions:

| Go straight |
| --- |
| *Allez tout droit* <br> *Continuez tout droit* |
| **Take a turn** |
| *Tournez à gauche / à droite.* |
| *Prenez à gauche / à droite.* |

| Take a street / avenue/ boulevard |
| --- |
| *Prenez la rue Emile Zola.* |
| *Prenez la première rue à gauche.* |
| *Montez la rue Emile Zola.* |
| *Descendez l'avenue Montaigne.* |

- To conjugate -RE verbs, we remove the -re ending and add the following: *-s, -s,* (none), *-ons, -ez, ent.*
- Certain -RE verbs are irregular, like *prendre*: *je prends, tu prends, il/elle/on prend, nous prenons, vous prenez, ils/elles prennent.*
- To form the imperative, we use the present tense conjugation of verbs in the pronouns *tu, vous* and *nous*. For -ER verbs, we form the imperative mood in the second person *tu* by removing the -s.

# Exercises

1-2. Complete the dialogue with the appropriate missing words:

- Bonjour Madame, où est la gare s'il vous plaît ?
- Continuez tout 1._____et prenez la première 2._____à droite.

3-4. Complete the dialogue with the appropriate missing words:

    Excusez-moi Monsieur, je 3.___l'hôpital ?
- 4._____à gauche, l'hôpital est en face du Café des Deux Moulins.

5-6. Conjugate the indicated verb in the present tense.

5. Je (descendre) _____ la rue Michelet.
6. Sophie et Lucas (prendre) _____ le train pour aller au travail.

7-10. Transform the following declarative sentences into commands, using the imperative mood.

7. *Tu tournes à gauche.*_____.
8. *Tu fais la lessive.*_____.
9. *Nous prenons le train.*_____.
10. *Vous montez la rue Louis Blanc.*
_____.

# Answer Key

1. droit
2. rue
3. cherche
4. Tournez OR Prenez
5. descends
6. prennent
7. Tourne à gauche.
8. Fais la lessive.
9. Prenons le train.
10. Montez la rue Louis Blanc.

# Chapter 16: Ready for an adventure

*Le plus beau voyage, c'est celui qu'on n'a pas encore fait.*

The most beautiful journey is the one we have yet to take.

- Loïck Peyron

Even the most spontaneous travelers take some time to plan for a trip. This means looking for accommodation and choosing which touristic activities to do and which spots to visit. If you wish to spend holidays in a French-speaking country then this chapter will prepare you for these essential tasks.

In this lesson, you will learn how to reserve a hotel room. We will also study how to describe the places you see.

## Reserving a room

To call for a reservation, we can use the following expressions:

- *Je voudrais faire une réservation.* I would like to make a reservation.
- *C'est pour une réservation.* It's for a reservation.
- *Je voudrais réserver une chambre.* I would like to reserve a room.

To indicate the date, duration and number of guests, you can say:

*Est-ce que vous avez de la place ce soir / lundi prochain / le 8 janvier ?*
Do you have a room tonight / next Monday / January 8.

*Je voudrais réserver une chambre pour une nuit / trois nuits / une semaine.*
I would like to reserve a room for one night / three nights / a week.

*C'est pour deux personnes.*
It's for two people.

*Nous sommes trois.*
We are three (guests).

You can also ask for additional information using the following expressions:

**Est-ce qu'il y a une télévision dans la chambre ?**
Is there a TV in the room?

**Est-ce qu'il y a du wifi dans la chambre ?**
Is there wifi in the room?

**Est-ce qu'il y a une piscine dans l'hôtel ?**
Is there a swimming pool in the hotel?

**Est-ce que le petit déjeuner est compris ?**
Is breakfast included ?

**À quelle heure est le petit déjeuner ?**
At what time is breakfast (served)?

**À quelle heure peut-on s'enregistrer dans la chambre ?**
At what time can we check in the room?

**À quelle heure doit-on libérer la chambre ?**
At what time is the check out? (lit. At what time must one free the room?)

## Hotel reservation vocabulary

|  | Translation |
|---|---|
| avec vue sur | with a view on |
| connexion (f.) wifi | wifi connection |
| des serviettes (f.) | towels |
| l'ascenseur (m.) | the elevator |
| la clé | the key |
| la réception | the reception |
| le numéro de la chambre | the room number |
| un lit double | a double bed |
| un lit simple | a single bed |
| un plan | a map |
| une chambre à deux lits | a twin bedroom |
| une chambre double | a double bedroom |
| une chambre simple | a single bedroom |

If you find yourself reserving a room *en ligne* (online) or *sur place* (on-site), these phrases will surely help:

**J'ai fait une réservation en ligne au nom de...**
I made a reservation online under the name...

**Je n'ai pas de réservation. Avez-vous une chambre disponible ?**
I don't have a reservation. Do you have a room available?

# Touring the city

Below, we list some common vocabulary related to tourism:

*Tourism vocabulary*

|  | Translation |
|---|---|
| *une location de voiture* | a car rental |
| *un dépliant* | a leaflet |
| *un guide touristique* | a tour guide |
| *un itinéraire* | an itinerary |
| *un logement* | a lodging, an accommodation |
| *un monument* | a monument |
| *un plan* | a map |
| *un vol* | a flight |
| *une agence de voyages* | a travel agency |
| *une brochure* | a brochure |
| *une carte* | a map |
| *une croisière* | a cruise |

## GRAMMAR TIP
### The pronoun y

Let's study an excerpt of a brochure:

**Cette place est la plus grande place de la ville. On y trouve la Statue du Petit Prince.** (This square is the biggest square in the city. One finds there the Statue of the Petit Prince.)

Notice how instead of repeating *cette place*, we replace it instead with the word *y*:

| | | |
|---|---|---|
| *On* **place** | *On trouve* **sur cette** → | *On* **y** *trouve la Statue du Petit Prince.* |

The pronoun *y*, as you may observe here, is used to replace a place. It can be roughly translated to the English "here" or "there". To specify, *y* replaces:

- places preceded by the prepositions *à*, *chez*, *dans*, *en* or *sur*.
- places that are implied though not specified.

Let's look at some examples:

- *Mathis joue* **au parc**. → *Mathis* **y** *joue.*
- *Je vais* **chez un ami**. → *J'***y** *vais.*
- *On se retrouve* **au café** ? → *On s'***y** *retrouve ?*
- *On* **y** *va?* ("Let's go?" – the destination here is implied).

Like the pronoun *en*, *y* is generally placed before the verb.

## Touristic activities

We list below some common touristic activities:

| | Translation |
|---|---|
| *faire du shopping* | to go shopping |
| *faire du tourisme* | to go sightseeing |
| *marcher* | to walk |
| *partir en vacances* | to go on vacation |
| *se baigner* | to go swimming |
| *se promener* | to go for a walk, to take a walk |
| *visiter le centre-ville* | to visit downtown |
| *visiter un musée* | to visit a museum |

# Describing tourist spots

### Demonstrative pronouns

There are many ways to describe a tourist spot. In Chapter 4, we learned how to use basic adjectives in French. Remember that they are generally placed after the noun. For example:

**Cette plage se trouve en Grèce.**
This beach is located in Greece.

When pointing to a specific noun, we use demonstrative pronouns. In English, for instance, we use "this" or "these" when referring to something near the speaker. In French, the demonstrative pronouns change according to gender and number. Let's look at some examples:

- **Ce château est magnifique !** This castle is magnificent!
- **Cet endroit est extraordinaire.** This place is extraordinary.
- **Cette ville est pittoresque.** This city is picturesque.
- **Ce quartier est très calme.** This neighborhood is very calm.

Study the table below:

|  | Demonstrative Pronoun |  |
|---|---|---|
| masculine, starts with a consonant | **ce** | **ce** parc, **ce** café |
| masculine, starts with a vowel or *h* | **cet** | **cet** endroit, **cet** hôtel |
| feminine | **cette** | **cette** église, **cette** école |
| plural | **ces** | **ces** parcs, **ces** écoles |

Note that before masculine nouns starting with a vowel, we use the variation *cet*, and not *ce*.

# Key Takeaways

- To make a hotel reservation, we use the following expressions:

| **Introduction** |
|---|
| *Je voudrais faire une réservation.* |
| *C'est pour une réservation.* |
| **Giving details** |
| *Est-ce que vous avez de la place ce soir / lundi prochain / le 8 janvier ?* |
| *Je voudrais réserver une chambre pour une nuit / trois nuits.* |
| *C'est pour deux personnes.* |
| *Nous sommes trois.* |

*Est-ce qu'il y a une télévision / du wifi dans la chambre ?*
*Est-ce qu'il y a une piscine dans l'hôtel ?*
*Est-ce que le petit déjeuner est compris ?*
*À quelle heure est le petit déjeuner ?*
*À quelle heure peut-on s'enregistrer dans la chambre ?*
*À quelle heure doit-on libérer la chambre ?*

- The pronoun *y* replaces places that are preceded by the prepositions *à*, *chez*, *dans*, *en* or *sur*. It also replaces places that are implied in the context.
- The demonstrative pronouns "this" and "these" in French are: *ce*, *cet*, *cette* and *ces*.

Up until now, we've only looked at verbs conjugated in the present tense form. In the next chapter, you will learn how to conjugate them in the composed past tense, to talk about past events. We will also study vocabulary related to holidays and traditions.

## Exercises

1-2. Complete the dialogue with the appropriate missing words:

- Bonjour Monsieur, est-ce que vous avez de la 1._____ce soir ?
- C'est pour combien de personnes ?
- Nous sommes deux.
- D'accord... Nous avons une 2._____à deux lits disponible.

3. Complete the dialogue with the appropriate missing words:

- 3._____le petit déjeuner est compris ?
- Oui Monsieur, le petit déjeuner est inclus dans le prix.

4-7. Replace the underlined noun with *y*, following the example.

ex. *Je vais <u>au parc</u>.* → __J'y vais .

4. Éric est <u>à la plage</u>._____.
5. Vous allez <u>en France</u> demain?_____.
6. Nous dînons <u>chez Jean</u>._____.
7. On achète des stylos <u>dans ce magasin</u>._____.

8-10. Complete the sentences with the appropriate demonstrative pronoun.

8. J'adore_____musée !
9. _____étudiant ne fait pas ses devoirs.

144

10. _____belles plages se trouvent en Thaïlande.

# Answer Key

1. place
2. chambre
3. Est-ce que
4. Éric y va.
5. Vous y allez demain ?
6. Nous y dînons.
7. On y achète des stylos.
8. ce
9. Cet
10. Ces

# Chapter 17: A thing of the past

*Le passé, c'est la lampe qui éclaire l'avenir.*

The past, it's the lamp that lights the future.

- Jean-Louis-Auguste Commerson

The holidays just ended. Your friends ask you what you did or how it was. And so, you tell them what meal you had or what gifts you received. And for some laughs, you even add a few funny anecdotes. You had a fun time. You realize this as you relive the past by describing what happened.

In order to relate events that have already taken place, you would need to master the past tenses (yes, plural). In French language learning circles, the past tenses have gained quite a reputation as a difficult subject. Of particular notoriety is choosing which kind of past tense to use in specific contexts. Don't fret, for by the time you finish this lesson, you will be able to talk about the past using the correct grammatical tense. We will also learn how to talk about holidays and traditions.

## Talking about the holidays

Camille describes how she spent Christmas:

> *Noël dernier, **je suis allée** chez ma grand-mère. **Il neigeait** fort le matin, donc **nous ne sommes pas sortis** de la maison. L'après-midi, **j'ai fait** un bonhomme de neige avec les enfants. Ma grand-mère **a préparé** beaucoup de plats : foie gras fait maison, canard à l'orange, noix de Saint-Jacques sautées à l'ail... **Elle a** aussi **fait** un gâteau, **c'était** délicieux ! Après le repas, **nous avons ouvert** les cadeaux. **J'ai reçu** des chaussures !*

Last Christmas, I spent Christmas at my grandmother's place. It was snowing heavily in the morning, so we didn't leave the house. In the afternoon, I made a snowman with the kids. My grandmother prepared a lot of dishes: homemade foie gras, duck à l'orange, sautéed scallops with garlic... She also made a cake, it was delicious! After the meal, we opened the presents. I got shoes!

Observe the highlighted phrases above. These are all in the past tense. In French, there are two grammatical tenses used to express the past: *le passé composé* (the composed past tense) and *l'imparfait* (the imperfect tense).

### Composed past tense

The composed past is used to relate:

- successive actions or events.
- actions or events that happened at a specific point of time.
- actions or events that happened suddenly.

We'll delve deeper into the uses of the composed past in a while, when we compare it to the imperfect tense.

For now, let's look at how the composed past is formed. The formula is:

*AVOIR* or *ÊTRE* IN PRESENT TENSE + PAST PARTICIPLE OF THE VERB

For example, in the sentence above — *Elle <u>a fait</u> un gâteau* (She made a cake) — we have the auxiliary verb *avoir* conjugated in the present tense (*a*), and the past participle of the verb *faire* (*fait*). Let's look at other examples:

- ***J'ai dansé toute la nuit.*** *I danced all night.*
- ***Nous avons regardé un film.*** *We watched a film.*
- ***Vous êtes allés à la bibliothèque** ? Did you go to the library?*

How do we know whether to use *avoir* or *être*? For most verbs, we use *avoir*. *Être* is used only with the following verbs:

| | |
|---|---|
| *aller* | to go |
| *arriver* | to arrive |
| *descendre* | to go down |

148

| | |
|---|---|
| *devenir* | to become |
| *entrer* | to go in |
| *monter* | to go up |
| *mourir* | to die |
| *naître* | to be born |
| *partir* | to leave, to go |
| *rentrer* | to go back, to come home |
| *rester* | to stay |
| *retourner* | to go back, to return |
| *sortir* | to go out |
| *tomber* | to fall |
| *venir* | to come |

Now that you know whether to choose *avoir* or *être*, all that's left is to add the past participle. To form the past participle, here are the rules to follow.

- For -ER verbs, change the ending to é. (ex. *manger* → *mangé* ).
- For -IR verbs, change the ending to i. (ex. *partir* → *parti*).
- For -RE verbs, change the ending to u. (ex. *descendre* → *descendu*).

Remember that these are general rules. And as we've painfully learned by now, there are some exceptions. For now, start with these basic rules and move forward after mastering them.

Here is one last thing to remember when forming the composed past. When the auxiliary verb used is *être*, the past participle agrees in gender and number with the subject. For feminine subjects, we add an -e. For plural subjects, we add an -s. Remember that this is not the case when we use *avoir*. And so, for example:

- *Hélène **est partie** tôt.* Hélène left early.
- *Hélène **a mangé** le sandwich.* Hélène ate the sandwich.

Notice that we change *parti* to *partie* because the subject is feminine. But, in the second sentence, since we're using *avoir*, the past participle does not change at all. Here are other examples:

- *Elle est déjà arrivée.* She already arrived.

- ***Nous sommes allés au parc.*** We went to the park.
- ***Léa et Claire sont rentrées tard.*** Léa and Claire came home late.

## The imperfect tense

The imperfect tense is used to relate:

- past descriptions (weather, time, feelings, etc.).
- events with no definite ending.
- actions or events that are repeated.
- simultaneous actions.

To form the imperfect tense, we take the present tense of the verb conjugated in *nous* form, and add specific endings. For example, let's look at the imperfect tense of *aimer* (to like). So, first we take the present tense conjugation of *aimer* in *nous*, which is *nous aimons*. And then, we remove -ons and replace them with these endings.

| (nous) aimons  →  *aim-* | | |
|:---:|:---:|:---:|
| **Je** | +ais | aim**ais** |
| **Tu** | +ais | aim**ais** |
| **Il/Elle/On** | +ait | aim**ait** |
| **Nous** | +ions | aim**ions** |
| **Vous** | +iez | aim**iez** |
| **Ils/Elles** | +aient | aim**aient** |

Let's look at another example. How about the verb *partir*? In present tense *nous*, we conjugate it as *nous partons*, and so:

| (nous) partons  →  *part-* | | |
|:---:|:---:|:---:|
| **Je** | +ais | part**ais** |
| **Tu** | +ais | part**ais** |
| **Il/Elle/On** | +ait | part**ait** |
| **Nous** | +ions | part**ions** |
| **Vous** | +iez | part**iez** |
| **Ils/Elles** | +aient | part**aient** |

*Avoir* and *être* have irregular conjugation. We follow the endings above, but the root is different. For *avoir*, it is av- :

|  | *avoir* |
|---|---|
| **J'** | avais |
| **Tu** | avais |
| **Il/Elle/On** | avait |
| **Nous** | avions |
| **Vous** | aviez |
| **Ils/Elles** | avaient |

For *être*, it's ét- :

|  | *être* |
|---|---|
| **J'** | étais |
| **Tu** | étais |
| **Il/Elle/On** | était |
| **Nous** | étions |
| **Vous** | étiez |
| **Ils/Elles** | étaient |

### Composed past vs. imperfect

Now that you know how to form these two tenses, you need to learn when to use them. Above, we've listed the uses of each. Let's look at them again, but this time with examples:

| Composed past tense | Imperfect tense |
|---|---|
| • successive actions or events<br><br>*J'ai fait les courses, j'ai cuisiné, puis j'ai mangé.* (I did the grocery, I cooked, then I ate.) | • past descriptions<br><br>*Il faisait beau. J'étais content.* (The weather was nice. I was glad.) |
| • actions or events that happened at a specific point of time<br><br>*La semaine dernière, je suis allé à Bordeaux.* (Last week, I went to Bordeaux.) | • events with no definite ending<br><br>*Je passais la journée devant la télé.*<br>(I was spending the day in front of the TV.) |
| • actions or events that happened suddenly<br><br>*J'ai reçu un appel.* (I received a call). | • actions or events that are repeated<br><br><br>*Tous les jours, je faisais du jogging.* (Everyday, I went jogging.) |
| | • simultaneous actions<br><br>*Je faisais la lessive pendant qu'il cuisinait.*<br>(I was doing the laundry while he was cooking.) |

An alternative way of thinking about the difference between these two is imagining a theatrical play. What happens in the background would be in the imperfect tense, while the main action would be the composed past.

**CULTURE TIP**
*Holidays in France*

A celebration in French is called *une fête*. Here are some of the traditional celebrations in France:

- *le 1ᵉʳ janvier, le jour de l'An* (New Year's)
- *le 14 février, la Saint-Valentin* (Valentine's Day)
- *le 22 mars – 25 avril, Pâques* (Easter)
- *le 1ᵉʳ mai, la fête du Travail* (Labor Day)
- *le 21 juin, la fête de la Musique* (Music Festival)
- *le 14 juillet, la fête nationale* (National Day)
- *le 1ᵉʳ novembre, la Toussaint* (All Saints' Day)
- *le 25 décembre, Noël* (Christmas)

A holiday, meaning those celebrations where we don't need to go to work (yippee!), is called *un jour férié*. Not all of the celebrations listed above are officially recognized as *férié*.

*Celebrations vocabulary*

|  | Translation |
| --- | --- |
| *Bonne année !* | Happy new year! |
| *des feux d'artifice* (m.) | fireworks |
| *fêter* | to celebrate |
| *Joyeux Noël !* | Merry Christmas ! |
| *un bouquet de fleurs* | a bouquet of flowers |
| *un cadeau* | a gift |
| *un sapin de Noël* | a Christmas tree |
| *une carte de vœux* | a greeting card |
| *une fête* | a party, a celebration |

# Key Takeaways

- To express the past in French, we use the composed past tense and the imperfect tense. The composed past is used to relate actions or events that are successive, that happened at a specific point of time, or that happened suddenly. The imperfect tense is used to relate past descriptions, events with no definite ending, or repeated and simultaneous actions.
- To form the composed past, we follow the formula: *avoir* or *être* in present tense + past participle of the verb.
- We use *avoir* for most verbs. We use *être* for the following verbs: *aller, arriver, descendre, devenir, entrer, monter, mourir, naître, partir, rentrer, rester, retourner, sortir, tomber* and *venir*.
- To form the past participle, we change the endings: ER becomes *é*, IR becomes *i* and RE becomes *u*.
- To form the imperfect tense, we take the present tense conjugation of the verb in *nous*, then replace the endings with: -*ais*, -*ais*, -*ait*, -*ions, -iez, -aient*.
- The verbs *avoir* and *être* have irregular conjugations in the imperfect tense. For *avoir*, the base is *av-* and for être, *ét-*.

In the final chapter of this book, we head to the future. You will learn how to talk about your future plans and your dreams.

## Exercises

1-3. Transform the indicated verbs into the composed past tense.

    1. Les enfants (manger)_____des bonbons.

    2. Le 1<sup>er</sup> janvier, la famille (aller)_____chez une amie.

    3. Nous (partir)_____en Suisse pour la Saint-Valentin.

4-6. Transform the indicated verbs into the imperfect tense.

    4. Quand on est arrivé, il (faire)_____mauvais.

    5. Jacques (chanter)_____.

    6. Je (avoir)_____un problème.

7-10. Composed past or imperfect tense? Conjugate the indicated verbs using the appropriate past tense.

Ce jour-là, il faisait beau. Nathan et ses enfants (aller) _____dans le parc. Ils (jouer)_____au foot. Les enfants (être)_____très heureux.

# Answer Key

1. ont mangé
2. est allée (because *la famille* is a singular, feminine noun.)
3. sommes partis
4. faisait
5. chantait
6. J'avais
7. faisait
8. sont allés
9. ont joué
10. étaient

# Chapter 18: The adventure continues

*L'avenir est une porte, le passé en est la clé.*

The future is the door, the past is its key.

- Victor Hugo

What better way to conclude your journey in learning beginner's French than to dream of a hopeful future? Being able to talk about the future is an important language skill to acquire. And we're not only talking about the big picture here, as in your career plans or projects. The future also plays a role in our daily lives.

We have mastered quite a lot of verb tenses since we started, some a bit more complicated than others. The great news is that the future tense is in fact one of the simplest conjugations you'll learn. In this chapter, we'll teach you how to describe your plans and how to express predictions.

## Plans and projects

There are two future tenses in French. "Not again!", we can hear you grumbling. But not to worry, the conjugation of these tenses is much more straight-forward than the past ones. The two future tenses are called *le futur proche* (near future) *and le futur simple* (simple future).

### Near future

The near future tense, called *le futur proche* in French, is used to talk about things that will certainly happen. It is also the more common, more informal of the two types of future tenses.

To form this tense, we simply add the verb *aller* (to go) in the present tense to the infinitive form of the verb. It's quite literally like the English verbal phrase "going to do something". For example, if you want to say, "I am going to eat with my friends", in French that would be:

*Je **vais manger** avec mes amis.*

So you have the present tense of *aller* (*vais*) which is added to the infinitive form of the main verb (*manger*).

Let's look at other examples:

- ***La famille va partir en vacances la semaine prochaine.*** The family will go on holidays next week.
- ***Vous allez fêter son anniversaire où ?*** You will celebrate his birthday where?
- ***Mes parents vont rentrer tard.*** My parents will come home late.

Quite simple right? Here's an added surprise: there are no exceptions to the rule. Finally!

---

### GRAMMAR TIP
***The present as future***

Take note that the present tense can also be used to talk about the future, especially when the event will happen soon. It's the same in English: you can say "The family <u>is going</u> on holidays next week." instead of "The family <u>will go</u> on holidays next week".

Similarly, in French, you can either use the present *La famille part en vacances*. Or the future, *La famille va partir en vacances.*

---

## Predictions and hypothesis

The next type of future tense is called *le futur simple*. This tense is mostly used to express plans in the distant future. It is more formal than the near future. Note as well that this tense is <u>not</u> as frequently used in conversations.


### Simple future

The simple future is used for predictions, like with the weather for example:

***Il y aura des nuages demain.***

It will be cloudy tomorrow (lit. There will be clouds tomorrow).

It is also used for hypothetical statements, especially with the relative pronouns *si* (if) and *quand* (when):

**S'il fait beau demain, j'irai au parc.**
If the weather is nice tomorrow, I will go to the park.

**Si tu t'entraines, tu seras plus fort.**
If you train, you will be stronger.

**Quand j'aurai le temps, j'apprendrai le français.**
When I have time, I will learn French.
**Quand je serai grand, je serai pilote.**
When I grow up, I will be a pilot.

To form the simple future, it's simple! We add the endings *ai*, *as*, *a*, *ons*, *ez* and *ont* to the infinitive form. Look at the table below:

| donner (to give) | | |
|---|---|---|
| **Je** | +ai | donner**ai** |
| **Tu** | +as | donner**as** |
| **Il/Elle/On** | +a | donner**a** |
| **Nous** | +ons | donner**ons** |
| **Vous** | +ez | donner**ez** |
| **Ils/Elles** | +ont | donner**ont** |

This is the rule for regular verbs, whatever their ending may be, -ER, -IR, or -RE.

There are some irregular verbs, like *avoir*, *être* and *aller*. For *avoir*, the base form is *aur-*, *ser-* for *être*, *fer-* for *faire*, and *ir-* for *aller*.

| avoir | être | faire | aller |
|---|---|---|---|
| *j'aurai* | *je serai* | *je ferai* | *j'irai* |
| *tu auras* | *tu seras* | *tu feras* | *tu iras* |

159

| | | | |
|---|---|---|---|
| *il/elle/on* aura | *il/elle/on* sera | *il/elle/on* fera | *il/elle/on* ira |
| *nous* aurons | *nous* serons | *nous* ferons | *nous* irons |
| *vous* aurez | *vous* serez | *vous* ferez | *vous* irez |
| *ils/elles* auront | *ils/elles* seront | *ils/elles* feront | *ils/elles* iront |

**CULTURE TIP**
*Expressions with venir*

We learned that the verb *venir* means to come. In French, the future is called *avenir*, which originally means *à venir* (to come, to happen). Here are some other expressions that use this verb:

- **dans les mois à venir** in the months to come
- **dans les années à venir** in the years to come
- **ça va venir** it will come, it will happen

# Key Takeaways

- There are two future tenses in French. The near future is used to talk about events that will certainly happen in the near future. The simple future is used to express predictions and hypotheses in the distant future. Of the two, the near future is less formal and used more often.
- The present tense can also be used to indicate future events.
- To form the near future, we add the present tense of the verb *aller* to the infinitive form of the main verb.
- To form the simple future, we add the following endings to the infinitive form of the verb : *-ai, -as, -a, -ons, -ez* and *-ont*.
- The verb *avoir* is irregular, its base form (to which we will add the endings) is *aur-*.
- For *être*, the base form is *ser-*.
- For *aller*, the base form is *ir-*.

*Bien joué !* Well done for getting this far! This may be the final chapter of this book, but it's not yet the end! Don't forget to review what you've learned by checking the vocabulary lists and verb conjugations in the annex.

## What's next

As this chapter's title says, the adventure continues! And not to worry, for we are right there with you. If you want to take your French further, you'll find it ideal to follow through with the next book in our series: ***Learn Intermediate French for Adults Workbook***. With this book, you will be able to build on what you learned here and achieve an intermediate level of fluency in French. We will look at longer conversations, more complex topics and more nuanced vocabularies, all with the same simplicity and clarity that this present book offers. *À bientôt l'aventurier*, see you soon adventurer!

## Exercises

1-5. Transform the indicated verbs into the near future tense.

> 1. Je (acheter)_____cette chemise.
> 2. Martin et ses amis (regarder)_____le match de foot ce week-end.
> 3. On (partir)_____de la maison à 9h.
> 4. Vous (prendre)_____ l'ascenseur ?
> 5. Mes collègues (organiser) _____ une fête de départ.

6-10. Transform the indicated verbs into the simple future tense.

> 6. Plus tard, je (avoir)_____une grande maison.
> 7. Dans dix mois, Christelle (quitter)_____ce travail.
> 8. Il (faire) _____ beau la semaine prochaine.
> 9-10. Quand je (être)_____ en France, je (passer) _____ mes journées dans les musées.

# Answer Key

1. vais acheter
2. vont regarder
3. va partir
4. allez prendre
5. vont organiser
6. j'aurai
7. quittera
8. fera
9. serai, passerai

# Vocabulary Lists by Theme

## *Greetings and basic expressions*

| | |
|---|---|
| Bye | *Salut* |
| Excuse me | *Excusez-moi* |
| Good evening | *Bonsoir* |
| Good night | *Bonne nuit* |
| Goodbye | *Au revoir* |
| Have a good afternoon | *Bon après-midi* |
| Have a good day | *Bonne journée* |
| Have a good day's end | *Bonne fin de journée* |
| Have a good evening | *Bonne soirée* |
| Hello, Bye | *Salut* |
| Hello, Good day | *Bonjour* |
| Hi | *Coucou* |
| No | *Non* |
| Pardon me, Excuse me | *Pardon* |
| Please | *S'il vous plaît* |
| See you in a bit | *À tout à l'heure* |
| See you in a moment | *À tout de suite* |
| See you later | *À plus (inf.), À plus tard* |
| See you soon | *À bientôt* |
| See you tomorrow | *À demain* |
| Thank you (very much) | *Merci (beaucoup)* |
| Until next time | *À la prochaine* |
| Yes | *Oui* |

## *Professions*

| | |
|---|---|
| an actor | *un acteur / une actrice* |
| a baker | *un boulanger / une boulangère* |

| | |
|---|---|
| a carpenter | *un charpentier / une charpentière* |
| a civil servant | *un/une fonctionnaire* |
| a cook | *un chef / une cheffe* |
| a dentist | *un/une dentiste* |
| a doctor | *un/une médecin* |
| an employee | *un/une employé(e)* |
| an engineer | *un/une ingénieur(e)* |
| a nurse | *un infirmier / une infirmière* |
| a police officer | *un policier / une policière* |
| a teacher | *un/une enseignant(e)* |
| a waiter | *un serveur / une serveuse* |

## *Nationalities*

| | |
|---|---|
| American | *américain(e)* |
| Austrian | *autrichien(ne)* |
| Belgian | *belge* |
| Canadian | *canadien(ne)* |
| Chinese | *chinois(e)* |
| English | *anglais(e)* |
| French | *français(e)* |
| German | *allemand(e)* |
| Greek | *grec(que)* |
| Japanese | *japonais(e)* |
| Korean | *coréen(ne)* |
| Mexican | *mexicain(e)* |
| Moroccan | *marocain(e)* |
| Portuguese | *portugais(e)* |
| Russian | *russe* |
| Spanish | *espagnol(e)* |
| Swede | *suédois(e)* |
| Vietnamese | *vietnamien(ne)* |

## Countries

| | |
|---|---|
| Algeria | *l'Algérie (f.)* |
| Australia | *l'Australie (f.)* |
| Austria | *l'Autriche (f.)* |
| Belgium | *la Belgique* |
| Brazil | *le Brésil* |
| Brunei | *le Brunéi* |
| Bulgaria | *la Bulgarie* |
| Cambodia | *le Cambodge* |
| Cameroon | *le Cameroun* |
| Canada | *le Canada* |
| Colombia | *la Colombie* |
| Congo | *le Congo* |
| Czech Republic | *la République tchèque* |
| Denmark | *le Danemark* |
| Egypt | *l'Égypte (f.)* |
| England | *l'Angleterre (f.)* |
| Finland | *la Finlande* |
| France | *la France* |
| Gabon | *le Gabon* |
| Gambia | *la Gambie* |
| Germany | *l'Allemagne (f.)* |
| Greece | *la Grèce* |
| Haiti | *Haïti* |
| Hungary | *la Hongrie* |
| Iceland | *l'Islande (f.)* |
| India | *l'Inde (f.)* |
| Indonesia | *l'Indonésie (f.)* |
| Iran | *l'Iran (f.)* |
| Iraq | *l'Irak (f.)* |
| Ireland | *l'Irlande (f.)* |
| Israel | *Israël (m.)* |
| Italy | *l'Italie (f.)* |

| Japan | le Japon |
| Malaysia | la Malaisie |
| Mexico | le Mexique |
| Morocco | le Maroc |
| Netherlands | les Pays-Bas |
| New Zealand | la Nouvelle-Zélande |
| Norway | la Norvège |
| Poland | la Pologne |
| Portugal | le Portugal |
| Russia | la Russie |
| Saudi Arabia | l'Arabie saoudite (f.) |
| Scotland | l'Écosse (f.) |
| Slovakia | la Slovaquie |
| Slovenia | la Slovénie |
| South Africa | l'Afrique du Sud (f.) |
| South Korea | la Corée du Sud |
| Spain | l'Espagne (f.) |
| Sri Lanka | le Sri Lanka |
| Switzerland | la Suisse |
| Thailand | la Thaïlande |
| United Arab Emirates | les Émirats arabes unis (m.) |
| United Kingdom | le Royaume-Uni |
| United States | les États-Unis (m.) |
| Vietnam | le Viêt Nam |

## School objects

| a backpack | un sac à dos |
| a bag | un sac |
| a book | un livre |
| a chair | une chaise |
| a computer | un ordinateur |
| a laptop | un ordinateur portable |
| a mobile phone | un (téléphone) portable |
| a notebook | un cahier |

| a pen | *un stylo* |
| a pencil | *un crayon* |
| a ruler | *une règle* |
| a table | *une table* |
| a whiteboard | *un tableau blanc* |

## *Basic adjectives*

| beautiful | *beau/belle* |
| big | *grand/grande* |
| black | *noir/noire* |
| cheap | *bon marché* |
| difficult | *difficile* |
| easy | *facile* |
| expensive | *cher/chère* |
| happy | *heureux/heureuse* |
| heavy | *lourd/lourde* |
| kind | *gentil/gentille* |
| light | *léger/légère* |
| long | *long/longue* |
| mean | *méchant/méchante* |
| sad | *triste* |
| short | *court/courte* |
| small | *petit/petite* |
| strong | *fort/forte* |
| ugly | *laid/laide* |
| weak | *faible* |
| white | *blanc/blanche* |

## *Numbers*

| 0 | *zéro* | 40 | *quarante* | 80 | *quatre-vingts* |
| 1 | *un* | 41 | *quarante et un* | 81 | *quatre-vingt-un* |
| 2 | *deux* | 42 | *quarante-deux* | 82 | *quatre-vingt-deux* |

| 3 | trois | 43 | quarante-trois | 83 | quatre-vingt-trois |
|---|---|---|---|---|---|
| 4 | quatre | 44 | quarante-quatre | 84 | quatre-vingt-quatre |
| 5 | cinq | 45 | quarante-cinq | 85 | quatre-vingt-cinq |
| 6 | six | 46 | quarante-six | 86 | quatre-vingt-six |
| 7 | sept | 47 | quarante-sept | 87 | quatre-vingt-sept |
| 8 | huit | 48 | quarante-huit | 88 | quatre-vingt-huit |
| 9 | neuf | 49 | quarante-neuf | 89 | quatre-vingt-neuf |
| 10 | dix | 50 | cinquante | 90 | quatre-vingt-dix |
| 11 | onze | 51 | cinquante et un | 91 | quatre-vingt-onze |
| 12 | douze | 52 | cinquante-deux | 92 | quatre-vingt-douze |
| 13 | treize | 53 | cinquante-trois | 93 | quatre-vingt-treize |
| 14 | quatorze | 54 | cinquante-quatre | 94 | quatre-vingt-quatorze |
| 15 | quinze | 55 | cinquante-cinq | 95 | quatre-vingt-quinze |
| 16 | seize | 56 | cinquante-six | 96 | quatre-vingt-seize |
| 17 | dix-sept | 57 | cinquante-sept | 97 | quatre-vingt-dix-sept |
| 18 | dix-huit | 58 | cinquante-huit | 98 | quatre-vingt-dix-huit |
| 19 | dix-neuf | 59 | cinquante-neuf | 99 | quatre-vingt-dix-neuf |
| 20 | vingt | 60 | soixante | 100 | cent |
| 21 | vingt et un | 61 | soixante et un | 1 000 | mille |
| 22 | vingt-deux | 62 | soixante-deux | million | million |
| 23 | vingt-trois | 63 | soixante-trois | billion | milliard |
| 24 | vingt-quatre | 64 | soixante-quatre | | |
| 25 | vingt-cinq | 65 | soixante-cinq | | |
| 26 | vingt-six | 66 | soixante-six | | |
| 27 | vingt-sept | 67 | soixante-sept | | |
| 28 | vingt-huit | 68 | soixante-huit | | |
| 29 | vingt-neuf | 69 | soixante-neuf | | |
| 30 | trente | 70 | soixante-dix | | |
| 31 | trente et un | 71 | soixante-et-onze | | |
| 32 | trente-deux | 72 | soixante-douze | | |
| 33 | trente-trois | 73 | soixante-treize | | |
| 34 | trente-quatre | 74 | soixante-quatorze | | |
| 35 | trente-cinq | 75 | soixante-quinze | | |
| 36 | trente-six | 76 | soixante-seize | | |

| 37 | trente-sept | 77 | soixante-dix-sept |
|----|-------------|----|-------------------|
| 38 | trente-huit | 78 | soixante-dix-huit |
| 39 | trente-neuf | 79 | soixante-dix-neuf |

## _Family_

| an aunt | une tante |
|---------|-----------|
| a brother | un frère |
| a child | un enfant |
| a daughter | une fille |
| a family | une famille |
| a father | un père (papa) |
| a female cousin | une cousine |
| a granddaughter | une petite-fille |
| a grandfather | un grand-père (papy, papi) |
| a grandmother | une grand-mère (mamie) |
| a grandson | un petit-fils |
| a husband | un mari |
| a male cousin | un cousin |
| a mother | une mère (maman) |
| a nephew | un neveu |
| a niece | une nièce |
| a relative, a parent | un parent |
| siblings | des frères et sœurs |
| a sister | une sœur |
| a son | un fils |
| an uncle | un oncle |
| a wife | une femme |

## _Places in the city_

| an apartment | un appartement |
|--------------|----------------|
| a bank | une banque |
| a building | un bâtiment |

| a cinema | un cinéma |
| a city hall | une mairie |
| a coffee shop | un café |
| downtown | le centre-ville |
| a hospital | un hôpital |
| a hotel | un hôtel |
| in the city | en ville |
| a library | une bibliothèque |
| a shopping mall | un centre commercial |
| a market | un marché |
| a museum | un musée |
| a park | un parc |
| a parking | un parking |
| a post office | un bureau de poste |
| a restaurant | un restaurant |
| a school | une école |
| a subway station | une station de métro |
| a supermarket | un supermarché |
| a theater | un théâtre |
| a train station | une gare |
| a university | une université |

## Parts of the house

| a balcony | un balcon |
| a basement | un sous-sol |
| a bathroom | une salle de bains |
| a bedroom | une chambre |
| a garage | un garage |
| a house | une maison |
| a kitchen | une cuisine |
| a living room | un salon |
| an office | un bureau |
| a patio | une terrasse |

| a room | une pièce |
| a staircase | un escalier |
| toilets | des w.c. (m.plur.), des toilettes (f.plur.) |

## Hobbies

| cooking | la cuisine |
| dancing | la danse |
| fashion | la mode |
| gardening | le jardinage |
| music | la musique |
| painting | la peinture |
| reading | la lecture |
| singing | le chant |
| sports | le sport |
| traveling | le voyage |
| video games | les jeux vidéo |

## Sports and music

| to bike | faire du vélo |
| to box | faire de la boxe |
| to go horseback riding | faire de l'équitation |
| to go mountain climbing | faire de l'alpinisme |
| to play basketball | jouer au basket |
| to play cards | jouer aux cartes |
| to play drums | jouer de la batterie |
| to play football | jouer au foot |
| to play tennis | jouer au tennis |
| to play the guitar | jouer de la guitare |
| to play the piano | jouer du piano |
| to play the violin | jouer du violon |
| to play volleyball | jouer au volley |
| to ski | faire du ski |

| to swim | faire de la natation |
|---|---|

## Baked goods

| an apple turnover | un chausson aux pommes |
|---|---|
| a baguette | une baguette |
| a cake | un gâteau |
| a chocolate bread | un pain au chocolat |
| a chocolate cake | un gâteau au chocolat |
| a croissant | un croissant |
| a lemon pie | une tarte au citron |
| a pie | une tarte |
| a sandwich loaf | un pain de mie |
| a strawberry pie | une tarte aux fraises |
| a whole-wheat bread | un pain complet |

## Fruits, vegetables and meat

| a carrot | une carotte |
|---|---|
| a peach | une pêche |
| a pear | une poire |
| a potato | une pomme de terre |
| a tomato | une tomate |
| an apple | une pomme |
| an apricot | un abricot |
| an eggplant | une aubergine |
| an orange | une orange |
| a banana | une banane |
| beef | du boeuf |
| a broccoli | un brocoli |
| a cabbage | un chou |
| cherries | des cerises (f.) |
| chicken | du poulet |
| duck | du canard |

| | |
|---|---|
| garlic | *de l'ail* |
| grapes | *du raisin* |
| green beans | *des haricots verts (m.)* |
| lamb | *de l'agneau* |
| lemon | *un citron* |
| lettuce | *une salade* |
| meat | *de la viande* |
| mussels | *des moules (f.)* |
| an onion | *un oignon* |
| a pineapple | *un ananas* |
| pork | *du porc* |
| salmon | *du saumon* |
| seafood | *des fruits de mer* |
| a steak | *un steak* |
| a strawberry | *une fraise* |
| tuna | *du thon* |
| turkey | *de la dinde* |

## *Weather*

| | |
|---|---|
| fall | *l'automne* |
| hail | *la grêle* |
| a lightning | *un éclair* |
| the moon | *la lune* |
| rain | *la pluie* |
| a rainbow | *un arc-en-ciel* |
| snow | *la neige* |
| spring | *le printemps* |
| a star | *une étoile* |
| a storm | *une tempête* |
| summer | *l'été (m.)* |
| the sun | *le soleil* |
| a thermometer | *un thermomètre* |
| thunder | *le tonnerre* |

| winter | *l'hiver* |

## *Days and months*

| a day | *un jour* |
| a week | *une semaine* |
| a month | *un mois* |
| Monday | *lundi* |
| Tuesday | *mardi* |
| Wednesday | *mercredi* |
| Thursday | *jeudi* |
| Friday | *vendredi* |
| Saturday | *samedi* |
| Sunday | *dimanche* |
| January | *janvier* |
| February | *février* |
| March | *mars* |
| April | *avril* |
| May | *mai* |
| June | *juin* |
| July | *juillet* |
| August | *août* |
| September | *septembre* |
| October | *octobre* |
| November | *novembre* |
| December | *décembre* |

## *Daily activities*

| to drink coffee | *boire du café* |
| to eat | *manger* |
| to eat breakfast | *prendre le petit-déjeuner* |
| to eat dinner | *dîner* |
| to eat lunch | *déjeuner* |

| | |
|---|---|
| to fall asleep | *s'endormir* |
| to get dressed | *s'habiller* |
| to get ready | *se préparer* |
| to get up | *se lever* |
| to go home | *rentrer* |
| to go to bed | *se coucher* |
| to go to school | *aller à l'école* |
| to go to the university | *aller à l'université* |
| to go to the university | *aller à la fac (slang)* |
| to go to work | *aller au travail* |
| to put makeup on | *se maquiller* |
| to read the newspaper | *lire le journal* |
| to rest | *se reposer* |
| to shave oneself | *se raser* |
| to take a shower | *se doucher* |
| to undress | *se déshabiller* |
| to wake up | *se réveiller* |
| to watch TV | *regarder la télé* |

## *Time*

| | |
|---|---|
| afternoon | *l'après-midi* |
| always | *toujours* |
| early | *tôt* |
| evening | *le soir* |
| every Monday | *tous les lundis* |
| every month | *tous les mois* |
| every week | *toutes les semaines* |
| everyday | *tous les jours* |
| frequently, often | *fréquemment* |
| from time to time | *de temps en temps* |
| generally | *en général, généralement* |
| late | *tard* |
| later | *plus tard* |

| | |
|---|---|
| morning | *le matin* |
| once a week | *une fois par semaine* |
| rarely, seldom | *rarement* |
| right now | *maintenant* |
| sometimes | *parfois* |
| today | *aujourd'hui* |
| tomorrow | *demain* |
| twice a week | *deux fois par semaine* |
| usually | *d'habitude* |
| yesterday | *hier* |

## *Chores*

| | |
|---|---|
| to clean up, to organize | *ranger* |
| to do laundry | *faire la lessive* |
| to do the dishes | *faire la vaisselle* |
| to go grocery shopping | *faire les courses* |
| to take out the garbage | *sortir la poubelle* |
| to vacuum | *passer l'aspirateur* |

## *Social activities*

| | |
|---|---|
| a bar, a pub | *un bar* |
| a club | *une boîte de nuit* |
| a housewarming party | *une pendaison de crémaillère* |
| a party | *une fête* |
| an outing | *une sortie* |
| to attend a party | *assister à une fête* |
| to go clubbing | *aller en boîte* |
| to go to a restaurant | *aller au restaurant* |
| to have a drink | *prendre un verre* |
| to attend a concert | *assister à un concert* |
| to see a play | *voir une pièce de théâtre* |
| to dine | *diner* |

| | |
|---|---|
| to go out | *sortir* |
| to visit a museum | *visiter un musée* |
| to watch a football match | *assister à un match de foot* |
| to watch a movie | *voir un film* |

## *Dining*

| | |
|---|---|
| a carafe, a jug | *une carafe* |
| a dish | *un plat* |
| a drink | *une boisson* |
| a main dish | *un plat principal* |
| a set meal | *une formule* |
| a special, a set meal | *un menu* |
| appetizer | *une entrée* |
| the check, bill | *l'addition (f.)* |
| a dessert | *un dessert* |
| the dish of the day | *le plat du jour* |
| the menu | *la carte* |
| to choose | *choisir* |
| to order | *commander* |
| to pay | *payer* |
| to reserve | *réserver* |
| water | *l'eau (f.)* |

## *Directions*

| | |
|---|---|
| after | *après* |
| at the end of (the street) | *au bout de (la rue)* |
| at the intersection | *au carrefour* |
| at the stoplight | *au feu* |
| before | *avant* |
| on the avenue | *sur l'avenue* |
| on the boulevard | *sur le boulevard* |
| in the street | *dans la rue* |

| | |
|---|---|
| to be located at | *se trouver* |
| to cross | *traverser* |
| to go down | *descender* |
| to go to | *aller à* |
| to go until | *aller jusqu'à* |
| to go up | *monter* |
| to return | *revenir, retourner* |
| to take | *prendre* |
| to turn (left or right) | *tourner, prendre (à gauche ou à droite)* |
| to your left | *sur votre/ta gauche* |
| to your right | *sur votre/ta droite* |

## *Hotel reservation*

| | |
|---|---|
| a double bed | *un lit double* |
| a double bedroom | *une chambre double* |
| a map | *un plan* |
| a single bed | *un lit simple* |
| a single bedroom | *une chambre simple* |
| the room number | *le numéro de la chambre* |
| the elevator | *l'ascenseur (m.)* |
| the key | *la clé* |
| the reception | *la réception* |
| towels | *des serviettes (f.)* |
| twin bedroom | *une chambre à deux lits* |
| wifi connection | *connexion wifi* |
| with view of | *avec vue sur* |

## *Tourism*

| | |
|---|---|
| a brochure | *un dépliant* |
| a brochure | *une brochure* |
| a cruise | *une croisière* |
| a flight | *un vol* |
| a map | *un plan* |

| a map | une carte |
| a monument | un monument |
| a tour guide | un guide touristique |
| a travel agency | une agence de voyages |
| an accommodation | un logement |
| an itinerary | un itinéraire |
| a car rental | une location de voiture |
| to go for a walk, take a walk | se promener |
| to go on vacation | partir en vacances |
| to go shopping | faire du shopping |
| to go sightseeing | faire du tourisme |
| to go swimming | se baigner |
| to visit a museum | visiter un musée |
| to visit downtown | visiter le centre-ville |
| to walk | marcher |

## *Celebrations*

| a bouquet of flowers | un bouquet de fleurs |
| a Christmas tree | un sapin de Noël |
| a gift | un cadeau |
| a greeting card | une carte de vœux |
| a party, a celebration | une fête |
| fireworks | des feux d'artifice (m.) |
| Happy new year! | Bonne année ! |
| Merry Christmas ! | Joyeux Noël ! |
| to celebrate | fêter |

# Verb Conjugations

| | Present | Composed past | Imperfect | Simple future |
|---|---|---|---|---|
| **Être** **(to be)** | je  suis | J'ai été | J'étais | je serai |
| | tu es | tu as été | tu étais | tu seras |
| | il/elle est | il/elle a été | il/elle était | il/elle sera |
| | nous sommes | nous    avons été | nous étions | nous serons |
| | vous êtes | vous avez été | vous étiez | vous serez |
| | ils/elles sont | ils/elles    ont été | ils/elles étaient | ils/elles seront |
| **Avoir** **(to have)** | j'ai | j'ai eu | j'avais | j'aurai |
| | tu as | tu as eu | tu avais | tu auras |
| | il/elle a | il/elle a eu | il/elle avait | il/elle aura |
| | nous avons | nous    avons eu | nous avions | nous aurons |
| | vous avez | vous avez eu | vous aviez | vous aurez |
| | ils/elles ont | ils/elles    ont eu | ils/elles avaient | ils/elles auront |
| **Aller** **(to go)** | je vais | je suis allé(e) | j'allais | j'irai |
| | tu vas | tu es allé(e) | tu allais | tu iras |
| | il/elle va | il/elle    est allé(e) | il/elle allait | il/elle ira |
| | nous allons | nous sommes allé(e)s | nous allions | nous irons |
| | vous allez | vous    êtes allé(e)s | vous alliez | vous irez |
| | ils/elles vont | ils/elles    sont | ils/elles allaient | ils/elles iront |

allé(e)s

| | | | | |
|---|---|---|---|---|
| **Chanter (to sing)** | je chante | j'ai chanté | je chantais | je chanterai |
| | tu chantes | tu as chanté | tu chantais | tu chanteras |
| | il/elle chante | il/elle a chanté | il/elle chantait | il/elle chantera |
| | nous chantons | nous avons chanté | nous chantions | nous chanterons |
| | vous chantez | vous avez chanté | vous chantiez | vous chanterez |
| | ils/elles chantent | ils/elles ont chanté | ils/elles chantaient | ils/elles chanteront |
| **Choisir (to choose)** | je choisis | j'ai choisi | je choisissais | je choisirai |
| | tu choisis | tu as choisi | tu choisissais | tu choisiras |
| | il/elle choisit | il/elle a choisi | il/elle choisissait | il/elle choisira |
| | nous choisissons | nous avons choisi | nous choisissions | nous choisirons |
| | vous choisissez | vous avez choisi | vous choisissiez | vous choisirez |
| | ils/elles choisissent | ils/elles ont choisi | ils/elles choisissaient | ils/elles choisiront |
| **Connaître (to know)** | je connais | j'ai connu | je connaissais | je connaîtrai |
| | tu connais | tu as connu | tu connaissais | tu connaîtras |
| | il/elle connait | il/elle a connu | il/elle connaissait | il/elle connaîtra |
| | nous connaissons | nous avons connu | nous connaissions | nous connaîtrons |
| | vous connaissez | vous avez connu | vous connaissiez | vous connaîtrez |
| | ils/elles connaissent | ils/elles ont connu | ils/elles connaissaient | ils/elles connaîtront |
| **Descendre** | je descends | je suis descendu(e) | je descendais | je descendrai |

| (to go down) | tu descends | tu es descendu(e) | tu descendais | tu descendras |
|---|---|---|---|---|
| | il/elle descend | il/elle est descendu(e) | il/elle descendait | il/elle descendra |
| | nous descendons | nous sommes descendu(e)s | nous descendions | nous descendrons |
| | vous descendez | vous êtes descendu(e)s | vous descendiez | vous descendrez |
| | ils/elles descendent | ils/elles sont descendu(e)s | ils/elles descendaient | ils/elles descendront |
| **Devoir (to have to)** | je dois | j'ai dû | Je devais | Je devrai |
| | tu dois | tu as dû | tu devais | tu devras |
| | il/elle doit | il/elle a dû | il/elle devait | il/elle devra |
| | nous devons | nous avons dû | nous devions | nous devrons |
| | vous devez | vous avez dû | vous deviez | vous devrez |
| | ils/elles doivent | ils/elles ont dû | ils/elles devaient | ils/elles devront |
| **Écrire (to write)** | j'écris | j'ai écrit | j'écrivais | j'écrirai |
| | tu écris | tu as écrit | tu écrivais | tu écriras |
| | il/elle écrit | il/elle a écrit | il/elle écrivait | il/elle écrira |
| | nous écrivons | nous avons écrit | nous écrivions | nous écrirons |
| | vous écrivez | vous avez écrit | vous écriviez | vous écrirez |
| | ils/elles écrivent | lis/elles ont écrit | ils/elles écrivaient | ils/elles écriront |
| **Faire (to do)** | je fais | j'ai fait | je faisais | je ferai |
| | tu fais | tu as fait | tu faisais | tu feras |
| | il/elle fait | il/elle a fait | il/elle faisait | il/elle fera |

|  | | | |
|---|---|---|---|
| | nous faisons | nous avons fait | nous faisions | nous ferons |
| | vous faites | vous avez fait | vous faisiez | vous ferez |
| | ils/elles font | Ils/elles ont fait | ils/elles faisaient | ils/elles feront |
| **Partir (to leave)** | je pars | je suis parti(e) | je partais | je partirai |
| | tu pars | tu es parti(e) | tu partais | tu partiras |
| | il/elle part | il/elle est parti (e) | il/elle partait | il/elle partira |
| | nous partons | nous sommes parti(e)s | nous partions | nous partirons |
| | vous partez | vous êtes parti(e)s | vous partiez | vous partirez |
| | ils/elles partent | ils/elles sont parti(e)s | ils/elles partaient | ils/elles partiront |
| **Pouvoir (to be able to)** | je peux | j'ai pu | je pouvais | je pourrai |
| | tu peux | tu as pu | tu pouvais | tu pourras |
| | il/elle peut | il/elle a pu | il/elle pouvait | il/elle pourra |
| | nous pouvons | nous avons pu | nous pouvions | nous pourrons |
| | vous pouvez | vous avez pu | vous pouviez | vous pourrez |
| | ils/elles peuvent | ils/elles ont pu | ils/elles pouvaient | ils/elles pourront |
| **Prendre (to take)** | je prends | j'ai pris | je prenais | je prendrai |
| | tu prends | tu as pris | tu prenais | tu prendras |
| | il/elle prend | il/elle a pris | il/elle prenait | il/elle prendra |
| | nous prenons | nous avons pris | nous prenions | nous prendrons |
| | vous prenez | vous avez pris | vous preniez | vous prendrez |

| | | | | |
|---|---|---|---|---|
| | ils/elles prennent | ils/elles ont pris | ils/elles prenaient | ils/elles prendront |
| **Savoir (to know)** | je sais | j'ai su | je savais | je saurai |
| | tu sais | tu as su | tu savais | tu sauras |
| | il/elle sait | il/elle a su | il/elle savait | ii/elle saura |
| | nous savons | nous avons su | nous savions | nous saurons |
| | vous savez | vous avez su | vous saviez | vous saurez |
| | ils/elles savent | ils/elles ont su | ils/elles savaient | ils/elles sauront |
| **Venir (to come)** | je viens | je suis venu(e) | je venais | je viendrai |
| | tu viens | tu es venu(e) | tu venais | tu viendras |
| | il/elle vient | il/elle est venu(e) | il/elle venait | il/elle viendra |
| | nous venons | nous sommes venu(e)s | nous venions | nous viendrons |
| | vous venez | vous êtes venu(e)s | vous veniez | vous viendrez |
| | ils/elles viennent | ils/elles sont venu(e)s | ils/elles venaient | ils/elles viendront |
| **Voir (to see)** | je vois | j'ai vu | je voyais | je verrai |
| | tu vois | tu as vu | tu voyais | tu verras |
| | il/elle voit | il/elle a vu | il/elle voyait | il/elle verra |
| | nous voyons | nous avons vu | nous voyions | nous verrons |
| | vous voyez | vous avez vu | vous voyiez | vous verrez |
| | ils/elles voient | ils/elles ont vu | ils/elles voyaient | Ils/elles verront |
| **Vouloir (to want)** | je veux | j'ai voulu | je voulais | je voudrai |
| | tu veux | tu as voulu | tu voulais | tu voudras |
| | il/elle veut | il/elle a voulu | il/elle voulait | il/elle voudra |

| | | | |
|---|---|---|---|
| nous voulons | nous avons voulu | nous voulions | nous voudrons |
| vous voulez | vous avez voulu | vous vouliez | vous voudrez |
| ils/elles veulent | ils/elles ont voulu | ils/elles voulaient | ils/elles voudront |

Made in the USA
Las Vegas, NV
05 May 2024

89568411R00109